PUB WALKS
IN
Surrey

TWENTY FIVE CIRCULAR WALKS
AROUND INNS IN SURREY

Christopher Howkins

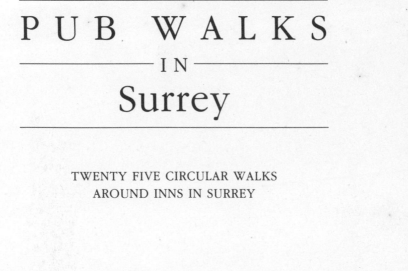

11th May 95.

To an active but boozy summer!

All love,

Tess

Happy Birthday!

COUNTRYSIDE BOOKS
NEWBURY, BERKSH

First Published 1992
© Christopher Howkins 1992
Revised and reprinted 1993, 1994

COUNTRYSIDE BOOKS
3 Catherine Road
Newbury, Berkshire

ISBN 1 85306 181 6

Cover illustration by Colin Doggett

Produced through MRM Associates Ltd., Reading
Typeset by Paragon Typesetters, Queensferry, Clwyd
Printed in England by J. W. Arrowsmith Ltd., Bristol

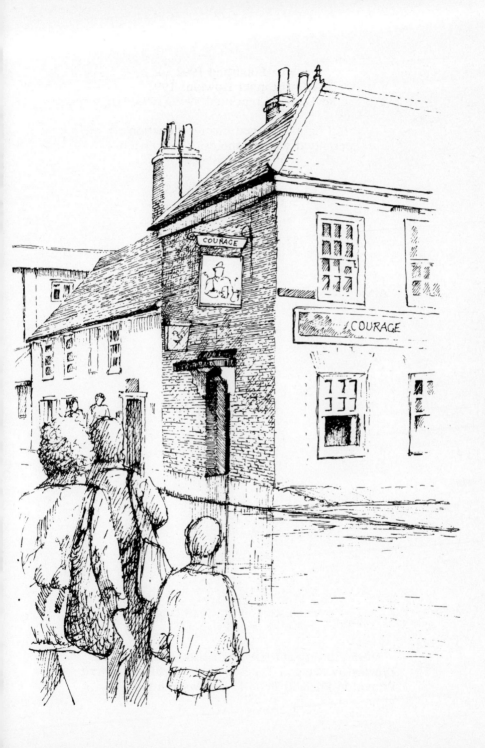

Contents

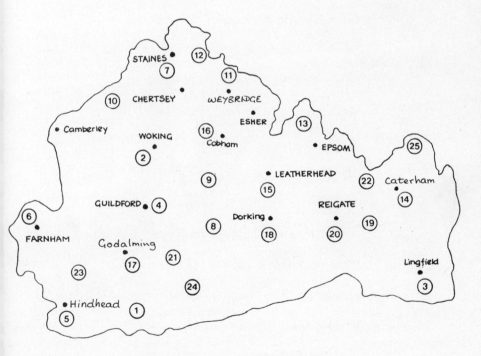

Area map showing locations of the walks.

Introduction

Surrey is a small county of enormous variety. Much of it is still farmland and woodland and heathland, all a far cry from television jokes that Surrey is no more than a car park for London. At least those comments deter many people from coming to see for themselves, leaving plenty of opportunities for a quiet ramble round a village and a drink in the local pub.

The towns and villages are just as varied as the landscape. There is no broad identity like the Cotswolds or East Anglia or the Yorkshire Dales, at least, not at first sight, but there is a 'Surrey style' which takes a little longer to recognise and savour.

With this in mind the rambles have been chosen to take in all the main landscape types from Thames Valley gravels to the chalk Downs, the sandy heathlands and the clay Weald. Some are for people to enjoy the rural setting and its wildlife while others include historic villages and towns.

Matching up locations with suitable pubs proved much more difficult than expected. Surrey has the reputation with outsiders of being snobbish and there are certainly pubs where ramblers are not welcome and display notices saying so. All pubs included in this book have declared ramblers are welcome. It does not of course mean that there will be a welcome for an unexpected horde of people with mud up to their ears! Common sense has to be used. In most pubs muddy boots and shoes are not welcome, and their presence can only damage the good reputation that walkers generally have.

Many of the routes chosen are mud free so the problem does not arise. Similarly family groups shouldn't find any problem but larger parties should phone first. There are no special 'ramblers' bars' as in some parts of the country.

Finding welcoming pubs was the first criteria. Then we selected those that could fuel a day out by offering reasonable sized meals (big enough to sustain a hungry researcher not on a diet!) at a reasonable price.

The information was provided by the pubs and so should be correct but of course landlords and services change. No pub paid to be included; no free meals or drinks were accepted. Not all the entries declare whether dogs and children are admitted and these reserve the right to use their discretion. The law forbids entry to dogs in places where food is prepared and served but if you are only using the bar area and the food area is separate your dog might be admitted. Similarly the law forbids entry to children less than 14 years old but again if it is for a meal and that meal is served in a separate area then pubs are admitting children. Not all pubs are so clearly defined and so if in doubt phone first.

Unless otherwise stated car parking is available at the pub but this is a facility for patrons of the pub and non-patrons will not only be unpopular if they leave cars there but could return to a heavy parking charge or find their car impounded or wheel clamped, especially in urban areas. For each ramble there is alternative parking nearby.

These excursions are designed for people to ramble round at leisure, allowing time to stop and look and photograph. They are not aimed at pleasing people who like to clock up miles and miles. Although some will appear very short remember the extra walking to explore churches and other sites of interest and of course hills will make them more tiring.

On the whole routes are clearly defined, avoiding those where landowners are known to obstruct. Wherever problems arise they should be reported to the Local Authority. Inevitably there are changes around the county but all routes included are believed to be public paths although a right of way can never be totally guaranteed.

Finally, many thanks are due to Daniel Powell for help in checking most of the routes and visiting the pubs; and to Darren Hemsley and Tim Laws for the sketch maps. They are only simple guides, not drawn to scale, and for the rural routes ramblers are strongly urged to use an Ordnance Survey map as well. The relevant OS Map Landranger Series is given for each walk. We wish all users many happy hours experiencing the pleasures of the varied little county that is Surrey.

Christopher Howkins

Dunsfold
The Sun Inn

The Sun Inn (Friary Meux) snuggles into the long grass at the back of the Common with the line of the Dunsfold village continuing on either side. It has a pleasing Georgian frontage but step inside and you'll find the left section is 17th century while the right end is 15th century with all the roof timbers exposed. This part was once a hop drying barn.

All are welcome at The Sun, with a garden and the Common outside for the children but parents note, there are several ponds dotted round the Common, all very inviting for little children.

There is an extensive menu to choose from and of the home-made meals the steak and kidney pie is so popular it is the one item never changed. There is a separate restaurant that can take group bookings for up to 20 diners and on some Sunday evenings in summer there is a barbecue.

Opening hours: 11 am-3 pm, 6 pm-11 pm Monday to Saturday; 12 noon-3 pm and 7 pm-10.30 pm Sunday.

Food served: 12 noon-2.15 pm and 7 pm-10 pm Monday to Saturday; 12 noon-2 pm and 7 pm-9.30 pm Sunday.

Telephone: 0483 200242.

How to get there: Dunsfold is just off the B2130 between Cranleigh and Chiddingfold.

Parking: Outside the pub on the Green.

Length of the walk: 2 miles. O.S. Map Landranger Series 186.

Dunsfold is one of the county's most remote villages, down on the edge of the Weald. The village green is known as the Common and is kept as a great long open space of rough grass, trees and bushes, which pushes one side of the village well back from the road so that even today it has the most wild and remote feel of any Surrey village. Once it was an industrial centre of the Wealden iron industry, with adjoining Chiddingfold the centre of glassmaking. All that has now gone to leave beautiful countryside to explore. This varied walk has plenty of interest, ranging from the early settlement around the church to the holy well and the mill, amid the fields and woods.

The Walk

On leaving The Sun turn left and follow the line of village homes and gardens along the fringe of the Common to the road at the end. One of the ponds, full of wild flowers, lies over the road.

Turn left and follow the lane up and over the hill and down into the dip.

Turn left for Church Green at the first junction and follow the narrow lane on its curl round the hill through the trees; sheltered in winter, cool in summer and a delight in spring with a ground flora of violets and wood anemones.

Church Green is soon reached – a tiny grassy area on the hillside with a few richly textured houses of brick and tile about it. It has been suggested that this was the site of the first settlement, probably of forest workers, when this was a remote corner of the manor of Bramley in the parish of Shalford. Clues come from the presence here of the church, ancient yew, holy well, mill and its proximity to a Roman route. The present village must have developed down on the Common later, perhaps in Tudor times.

The churchyard has the massive hollow yew tree, probably predating the church, and marking an ancient sacred spot. Yews are, however, notoriously difficult to date and not all large ones are as old as people would like to think. This one, well over 20 ft round, seems to be dying back.

The church is of national importance, not only for being a near complete building of about 1270 but for being of advanced design and superior workmanship. As Dunsfold was owned by the Crown at this time it is suggested that top royal masons from Westminster were involved; certainly this was not the work of the village builder.

Turn right on leaving the lychgate and take the footpath down through the trees to the river. This can be muddy in winter.

Cross the stile on the left to enter the field beside the holy well, which was formerly held in esteem for curing eye diseases. In 1933 the Dunsfold Amateur Dramatic Society had the little shrine built over it, designed by the local architect W.D. Caroe and dedicated by the Bishop of Guildford to the Blessed Virgin Mary. Unlike some counties, Surrey has only a couple of holy wells so this is quite a local rarity.

Follow the footpath left along the river bank through the field. (Keep dogs under control; there are often geese and horses here.)

Turn right at the driveway to cross the river. The hills behind Dunsfold pitch most of Surrey's water north to the Thames but from this southern edge it goes through the Weald to the English Channel. This slow deep-cut stream is the infant Arun heading for Arundel and the sea at Littlehampton. At this point stood Dunsfold Mill. It was a timber building enclosing the wheel but it was demolished long ago, leaving the wheel pit for the sharp-eyed to spot in the river.

Continue ahead towards the impressive mill house and turn left along the signposted footpath out across the field towards the trees. At the edge of the wood you cross the Arun again. The bridge has been rebuilt but incorporates the 1853 datestone from its predecessor (outside face of left parapet). This is a beautiful quiet spot that appears to be miles from anywhere.

Continue ahead up the hill through the wood (can be muddy in winter). Here, as through the previous field, there is a wealth of wildlife, trees and flowers to enjoy in due season.

Continue ahead at the road. Attention will now need to move to garden plants as a row of bungalows is passed.

Bear left with the housing onto the Common. There's another pond here, ringed with wild flowers in summer and full of goldfish.

Proceed round and The Sun Inn will soon be reached again.

Points of Interest

The church is a near perfect example of the practical simplicity of the Early English style in transition to the Decorated style, of 1270 to 1290. Building continued in the Decorated style until about 1350. The sedilia and piscina are outstanding; the wooden benches are the earliest in the country.

The belfry, like several others in Surrey, is supported upon massive beams. Sometimes, as at Byfleet, these were supported by the walls as the whole west end was raised in one build but here we can see the

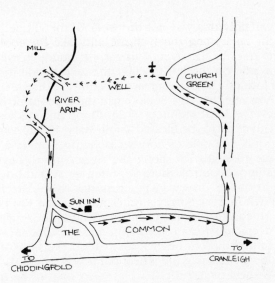

belfry was put in last and so four corner posts were necessary. It is a masterful piece of carpentry but it is not known by whom. However, at this time one of the great carpenters in royal service at Westminster was John Herland who is thought most likely to have come from Hurlande, here at Dunsfold, so perhaps it is his work.

Don't miss a peculiar rarity here. Along the base of the walls, best seen in the outside west or north wall, there are holes with wooden plugs on chains. These were drains from when the church floor was swilled down and may be the only examples left in the country. The plugs were to stop rats entering the church.

Pirbright
The White Hart

The White Hart (Ind Coope) is a very popular pub, able to cater for everyone. There is a separate family room and a large garden. Food ranges from three course evening meals, to hot meals at lunch time or quick snacks just to keep you going. Most of it is home-made. There is a separate restaurant for Thursday, Friday and Saturday nights, for which group bookings can be made for up to 32 diners (tel: 04867 2366). Large car park.

Opening hours: 12 noon-2-30 pm Monday to Friday; 11 am-2.30 pm Saturday; 12 noon-3 pm Sunday. Evenings: 6 pm-11 pm Monday to Saturday; 7 pm-10.30 pm Sunday.

Telephone: 0483 472366.

How to get there: Pirbright is on the A324 west of Woking and the White Hart overlooks the village green.

Length of the walk: 2 miles. O.S. Map Landranger Series 186.

The village is not as ancient as some. Initially it was probably a scattering of homesteads and so it did not warrant a separate entry in the Domesday Book of 1086 but the name was in use by 1166. It means 'the pear tree wood' and a wonderful fruiting pear tree creates the village sign on the green. It has been in the news several times, such as 13th September 1852 when Charles Green on his last balloon trip crashed into a bog on the common and terrified the villagers.

This ramble is partly by roadway and partly by field path, through trees and meadows, noting the old buildings on the way.

The Walk

From the White Hart there are views out over the green, with the village pond up on the right, the village hall centre distance and a very smart timber-framed house just across the road to the left.

Cross the main road to view this old house – mid 16th century and the oldest in the village. Originally a farmhouse, it has since served as the village grocery and butcher's shop and for long afterwards salt was said to ooze out of the walls from the days of bacon curing. Now it has been restored into a private dwelling.

Follow the lane in front of this house, away from the pub. The next old house is just as striking in its rosy red brick way. So much about it says it's a typical 17th century Surrey house but note the round-headed blocked central window and the cornice under the gutter, indicating the advent of Georgian-style architecture.

Before bearing round to the left, in front of another timber-framed house over the lane, there is the option of cutting across the green to the right of the village hall, where there is more of interest.

Bear left at the end of the green to follow Church Lane which is narrow and attractive.

Enter the graveyard through the gate on the right and follow the path ahead to the giant granite monolith which marks the burial place of Sir Henry Morton Stanley. Proceed ahead through the great copper beech and ancient oaks to find the church beyond. Being Georgian it is a great rarity in Surrey.

Exit via the south gate opposite the door and turn right. Now you are under more ancient oaks with a stream running by and views back to the church which make it look as though it's in a woodland clearing.

Follow the lane round to the left but before doing so try a detour to the right where a path runs beside the churchyard wall to bring you to a cottage on the left. A stone up in the cottage gable records that it was given to the church in 1929 as a memorial to Katherine Dalrymple

Halsey in recognition of her services to the parish.

Where the lane narrows, take the footpath on the left which runs through the field beside the road, keeping walkers safe (use the road if preferred) and cross the stile back into the lane at Appletree Cottage (note the farm is partly ancient with timber-framing).

Continue along the lane until it swings right and uphill and at that point take the footpath left. (Before doing so, it is worth diverting on ahead to the cottage that looks so attractive, especially when the old-fashioned roses are in bloom by the garden wall. This is Box Cottage which goes back to the 16th century. Although it has a broad frontage, walk on a bit and see how narrow it is under its wonderful catslide roof.)

Follow the footpath down to Hodge Brook, bridge that and cross the stile ahead into the meadow.

Don't turn aside but follow the path across the grass, up to the top of the odd little hill and cross the stile at the top. Continue ahead, following the ridge of the field. There are now long distance views out over West Surrey, to Kettlebury Hill with its scraggy pines on top and the more even line of pines on the skyline. Farnham lies in the valley beyond them.

Cross the stile at the end by the wall and look left down into the dip for one of those typically Surrey views of rooftops nestling under the flank of the hill.

Walk ahead through the larch wood, keeping the fence on the left. Turn left when the path meets the track – the footpath sign has a War Department numbered boundary marker stone at its base; military lands are close by so don't wander off! Note instead, Pirbright Lodge, built in 1774 by the grandfather of the poet Lord Byron. Complete

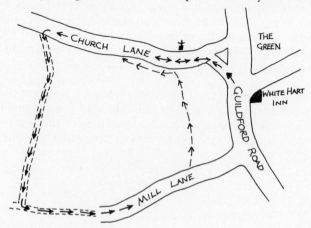

with stables it is a Grade II listed building.

Follow round to the left to the surfaced Mill Lane which leads back to Pirbright village centre, through a gentle landscape of green fields and trees. The sound of falling water heralds the proximity of Pirbright Mill, which can be glimpsed through the trees. It is now a private residence.

Next on the left is the ancient Manor which can again be glimpsed through the trees.

Now there is a choice – either continue down the lane to the main road and turn left to reach the White Hart on the next corner, or turn left off the lane just after the manor entrance and follow the path across the fields to the church and so back to the pub.

Points of Interest

Church and Churchyard Monolith to Sir Henry Morton Stanley, born John Rowlands in 1841 in Wales, who emigrated to America in 1859, changed his name and took US citizenship. He is best remembered for having been sent by the New York Herald to find Dr Livingstone, but was one of the great explorers of Africa, helping to found the Belgian Congo Free State, Uganda and Kenya – all commemorated on the monolith by the simple word 'Africa' and the name the Africans called him, 'Bula Matali'. At the end he resumed British nationality and served as a Liberal Unionist MP from 1895-1900. He spent the last six years of his life in Pirbright, at 'Furze Hill', till he died in 1904.

The church became ruinous and the parish too poor to restore it and so in 1783 George III sanctioned a national collection – see the transcript in the church. It was successful and rebuilding began the next year of a simple Doric church, so rare in Surrey. It is usually dated 1784 but the sharp-eyed can see it could not have been finished by then because in 1785 the workmen were still scratching their initials and dates on the bricks of the nave's south wall.

The manor dates from the 13th century when it was part of the great Honour of Clare and it stayed in noble hands. The old moat and the habitation platforms inside it are now features of the present garden but the oldest parts of the house we see are probably 16th century.

Lingfield
The Star

The Star (Whitbread) lies behind a large car park in Church Road. It has all the appearance of a 1930s Surrey pub complete with mock timbering in the front gable. Inside, old materials have been re-used to create an 'olde worlde' corner which is quite satisfying as the scheme has been underplayed. The pub is spacious and offers a tempting bistro menu that looks beyond England for its inspiration: most of the food is Mexican and Italian. For those who prefer the more traditional, there are ploughman's or a Sunday roast. The pub is open all day: 11 am to 11 pm, and for that, we were very thankful after our ramble in the heat.

Opening hours: 11 am-11 pm Monday-Saturday; 12 noon-3 pm; 7 pm-10.30 pm Sunday. Food served: 12 noon-2.30 pm; 6 pm (7 pm Sunday) to 9.30 pm.

Telephone: 0342 832364.

How to get there: The Star is situated just by the old Square in Lingfield.

Length of the walk: 4 miles. O.S. Map Landranger Series 187.

16

Lingfield, famous for its race course, is right down in the south-east corner of the county, on the Kent borders, in a flat agricultural landscape. The village was tiny until the railway came, bringing suburbia in its wake, but hidden in its heart is the beautiful late medieval square. Beside it stands the impressive church rebuilt in 1431 by Sir Reginald Cobham to serve the College he founded here. All around the village are fields and water meadows and open spaces with plenty of room to breathe. Therefore, ramblers have the choice here of either a sedate wander around the old church centre or a long peaceful walk through the fields and by the river.

The Walk

On leaving the pub cross the road to visit the delightful old square opposite. It's the scene that gets into all the picture books and no wonder. With its brick and tile, plaster and half timbering it's typical Surrey at its best but being drawn together here into a close coherent group creates a scene that is not at all common in the county. Note the 15th century open hall house on the left and in particular the plastered archways in the crosswing; these were shop fronts and such a find is difficult to repeat in Britain.

Move on to the church but don't fail to wander around the churchyard a bit, looking back at the Old Town Square because there are several very satisfying views that never seem to get into the books.

Leave by the north-east corner where there is a fine half-timbered building which was once the College guest house, and just for once you can see inside this one as it houses the County Library (2 pm-5pm Tuesday, Wednesday and Friday; 10 am-1 pm, 2 pm-5 pm Thursday; 9.30 am-1 pm, 2 pm-4 pm Saturday).

Walk down beside the library and turn right at the road. Cross Church Road to go down Bakers Lane, one of the quiet modern residential roads that make up so much of Lingfield. This is pleasant enough with its limes and horse chestnuts to add seasonal interest.

At the bottom, cross Station Road and go through the white gate to the level crossing. LISTEN for trains before crossing. Follow the farm track out through the fields and hedgerows in this flat agricultural landscape with the blue line of the Downs running along in the far distance. The river meandering so slowly and deeply through the pastures is the river Eden on its way to join the Medway over the Kent border.

Turn left at the farm and left again onto the signposted footpath. Cross the stile and continue ahead through the fields till you find a stile out of the field in the top left corner. Cross the gate in front of you. Through here the footpath route has been changed by statutory order and so maps are out of date. The waymarking arrow points diagonally right, across the fields to a gate by the riverbank where the lane

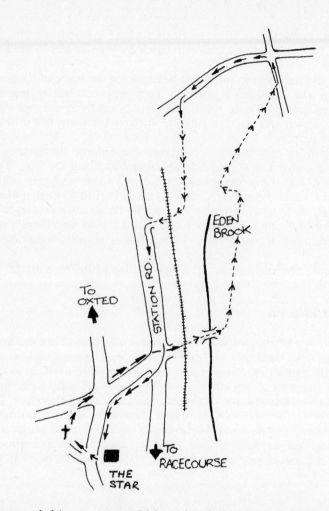

crosses and this we were told by a local farmer was correct.

Turn left along the surfaced lane to the T-junction ahead and turn left (but by turning right the great timber mill at Haxted is a few minutes away and this is opened as a watermill museum).

Follow the lane to the next junction. This is just over a mile and many ramblers will no doubt enjoy being able to forget about where they're putting their feet and appreciate this quiet country lane through the farmland. The trees and the proximity of the river encourage birds and the wayside flowers are good too. Bear left at the junction and after a few yards it bridges the river.

Turn left immediately after the bridge where a stile leads into the field. The footpath sign is a concrete block by your ankles in the long grass.

Follow the path across the fields heading for the spire of Lingfield church on the horizon. It looks a long way off but is reached surprisingly quickly! There will be the field boundaries on your right along this stretch and where a ridge with thorn trees juts out into the field is the exit.

Turn right out of the field, on the path through the thorn trees, to the level crossing. LOOK and LISTEN before crossing the line. Walk ahead out of the residential close on the other side and turn left to head for the village centre. Attention now has to turn to garden plants as this short last stretch is mainly residential. Some of the cottages go back to the post-railway development days of 1888 and there's also the old malt house, partly half-timbered and suitably long for its purpose.

Turn right up Bakers Lane and you are back on the start of the ramble.

Points of Interest

The church is a Surrey treasure house for its collection of late medieval furnishings and fittings – screens and monuments, stalls and misericords, font cover, brasses etc. The architecture itself, in simple Perpendicular style, is equally noteworthy although it does not have the rich decoration of some of the nation's great wool churches. The monuments to the Lords Cobham and their ladies are undoubtedly fine and Surrey has so few other examples of such tomb sculptures. In particular note the little Saracen, complete with turban and slippers, carved at the feet of one of the knights. There is a guide book in the church.

Compton
The Withies Inn

The Withies Inn is in a quiet setting off the main street of Compton but it can still be very busy as there is a welcome for everyone. There is on-site parking with extra parking at the rear.

Food, from a wide ranging menu, including home-made meals, is served daily 12 noon-1.45 pm and 7 pm-9.30 pm Monday to Saturday. There is a separate restaurant. Patrons are requested not to eat their own food on the premises.

Opening hours: Monday-Saturday 10.30 am-3 pm; 6 pm-11 pm. Sunday 12 noon-2 pm; 7 pm-10.30 pm.

Telephone: 0483 421158.

How to get there: Signposting is clear from the A3, A31 and from the Godalming direction.

Length of the walk: 2¼ miles. O.S. Map Landranger Series 186.

Compton village is both historic and very attractive, without modern development around it. The setting is still rural, below the southern flank of the Hog's Back chalk ridge to the west of Guildford. It is close enough to the town to be convenient for a pub visit and a ramble but at the same time not so close as to be spoiled by it. There are opportunities for comfortable wanders along the old street or for something more demanding in the surrounding district.

This is a varied rural expedition despite being so close to Guildford town centre. It's all by footpath with short stretches of country lane, through woods and fields over sandstone to the chalk ridge behind, taking in a length of the North Downs Way.

The Walk

Turn right out of the pub to follow the surfaced lane ahead through the trees to the first road junction.

Bear right at the junction and follow the lane right on up to the Coach House/Polsted Manor, after which the route forks. Fork left up the sandy path which becomes a gully and then quite a steep gully as you press ahead up into the flanks of the Downs above the village. It is not very far before the path reaches a junction with the North Downs Way.

Turn left to follow the North Downs Way which goes immediately downhill and between the farm buildings ahead. For a short stretch you will be aware of the main A3 on your right but from this you turn away at the road. Turn left at the road (sign on right for the Watts Gallery).

Before proceeding further decide whether to continue on the country ramble or to stay on this lane to visit the Watts Chapel and so through to the village street (turn left at the end of the lane).

For the country ramble turn left onto a footpath round the corner, after about 30 yards. It goes up steeply, down steeply and then there's a stile to cross. The path winds along with a house and garden well below its level, on the right. Pass the farm on the right and then cross a stile onto a concrete road.

Proceed ahead along the concrete roadway from farm buildings. Look for a stile on the right and cross it; signposted public footpath. There are two options here – don't cross the next stile but follow the other path round to the right beside the wooden post and rail fence.

Follow the path through the woods to the road. Turn left along the road which returns you to the beginning of the ramble, and so turn right to return to The Withies.

Points of Interest

The Watts Gallery houses works by, and in the former house of, the artist George Frederick Watts, 1817-1904. He became an RA in 1867 and became a well-known Victorian artist – one of the last grand allegorical history painters. He refused twice to accept a baronetcy but

21

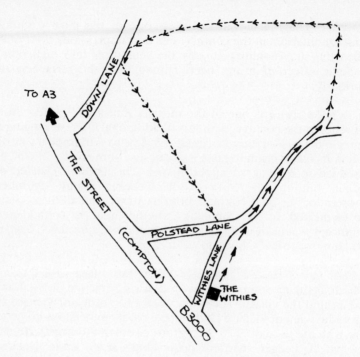

did accept the Order of Merit. It's his life rather than his work that seems to attract most attention nowadays. At 47 he decided to marry a wild spirited girl of 16 and rescue her from a stage career; he failed and so did the marriage after three years, leaving Ellen Terry to continue earning fame on the boards. Five years later he met another 16 year old who was to become his second wife but this time he waited 20 years. He was 69 by then. She adored him and built the incredible chapel to his memory. The Watts Gallery houses about 140 of Watts' paintings, a few pieces of sculpture and a few works by other contemporary artists. Open Wednesdays 2 pm-6 pm; 2 pm-4 pm October to March. Wednesday and Saturday mornings 11 am-1 pm.

The Watts Mortuary Chapel was designed and built by Mrs Watts, before her husband was dead, with help from villagers working as an arts-and-crafts movement. Visitors soon realise what that means for the whole building is highly decorated. Externally it looks Romanesque but closer inspection reveals the sculptural details to be of Celtic inspiration and the whole twined together in an attempt to be Art

Nouveau. That's achieved inside – one of the most exciting Art Nouveau interiors in the country. For best impressions do try to visit when the sun is shining to cast the sculptures into high relief for dramatic effect. If it has been raining then the terracotta shines gloriously.

The parish church is one of the most beautiful and perfect Norman churches in the country, with lots of additional interest, ranging from a precious piece of very early stained glass to a triumphant Jacobean pulpit. Its major claim to fame is the design of the east end which was extended to include an upper chapel. This is often claimed to be unique but there are two other double storey churches in Christendom – both Norman, both in Austria and all three churches are dedicated to St. Nicholas (whether that is coincidence or significant is not known). There is a guide book available inside and the church is usually open to visitors.

White Hart Cottage, a little way down the village street from the church, is the most interesting of the many attractive old buildings in and around the village. The white hart was a badge of Richard II but it's in the reign of Richard III that local royal connections come to the fore with the Lord of Field Place (further down the street). He was Sir Thomas St. Ledger, married to the king's sister, Anne, Duchess of Exeter, who became the local leader of insurrection for which he was executed as a traitor. White Hart Cottage may have no direct royal connection but it was certainly built far better than other local timber-framed buildings. When so few of those had any foundations at all this one was built on a substantial stone walled base. Up above, the timber framing was designed with the rare distinction for West Surrey of having two projecting storeys. It was a very grand house.

Thursley
The Three Horseshoes

The pub peeps out from under trees and wisteria by the road linking the A3 with the village street. There is car parking off the road and a vast garden (1½ acres) at the back for children and dogs. There are no fruit machines etc at the request of the locals so there is just country quiet and sociable chat to eat by whether in the bar area or in the separate restaurant.

There used to be a brass plate on the front wall forbidding ramblers but things have changed. It has been taken down and now everyone is welcome but rambling groups exceeding 5 are asked to notify the pub in advance. There is a friendly welcome, good service, an extensive menu and meals are excellent value for money. It is a freehouse with Gale's and Fuller's beers on offer.

Opening hours are Monday to Thursday 11 am-2.30 pm, Friday and Saturday 11 am-3 pm, Sunday 12 noon-3 pm. Evenings Monday to

Saturday 6 pm-11 pm, Sunday 7 pm-10.30 pm. Food all week 12 noon-2 pm; Monday to Thursday 7 pm-9 pm; Friday and Saturday 7 pm-9.30 pm.
Telephone: 0252 703268.

How to get there: Thursley hides in the folds of the hills at the mouth of the Devil's Punch Bowl, just west of the busy A3, below Hindhead. The central village of the district is Thursley with its winding street up past the Saxon church and so to The Devil's Punch Bowl. The only pub is The Three Horseshoes.

Length of the walk: 3 miles. O.S. Map Landranger Series 186.

The area was once more of a heathland setting with more sheep than people but with the decline in sheep grazing the trees have grown up to create a setting that is becoming increasingly wooded. However, conservationists are maintaining the famous lowland peat bog of European importance. The National Trust preserves thousands of acres of the surrounding countryside with free access at all times so there is no shortage of routes to ramble.

This relaxing walk takes in the village street and Saxon church before looping round through the attractive surrounding countryside, partly by lane and partly by footpath.

The Walk

Turn left on leaving the Three Horseshoes and walk down to the junction to turn left. On the right is the house where Sir Edwin Lutyens lived in his youth. His mother and nephew Derek are buried in Thursley.

Turn left and follow the lane that is the village street, if it can be called that; there are no shops nor a focal point along here. There isn't even very much traffic as it is not a through road. There are glimpses out over the fields and woods, between housing of various ages, the most attractive of which are up the top end where the lane bears right to rise up the hill to the church.

The church has Anglo-Saxon work of great interest, plus impressive woodwork and notable stained glass with smaller items of interest in a building recently redecorated and smartly maintained.

The churchyard has lost its famous horse chestnut tree but retains the Sailor's Stone. Notice the wooden 'shed' in the corner; it was once the village Dame School.

Opposite the church there has always been a good collection of weatherboarded barns behind the walls but now this area has been opened up and the barns can be more clearly seen. They are in a decayed state but will hopefully be restored as Surrey is losing many such examples of its vernacular architecture.

Above the church the house has an impressive brick frontage of the Georgian period. The proportions are too long though and a look at the side from the churchyard will show why. The frontage is nothing more than a facade to disguise a timber-framed Tudor farmhouse when such things became unfashionable. This being a particularly striking example, it occurs in a number of architecture books.

Continue right up the lane to the junction at the top. This is a walk between banks and high hedges, beautiful with Queen Anne's Lace in spring. You don't need to go to Devon to enjoy such narrow lanes.

Turn right at the junction at the top, where the lane becomes a dirt track into the Devil's Punch Bowl. For anyone wanting a longer ramble this is a good place to branch off, otherwise head for the cottage.

Turn right before the cottage to plunge very steeply down a path under the trees into a deep and mysterious hollow. Such is the scenery that features in the works of such local writers as Monica Edwards and S. Baring Gould. The latter is best known for writing the hymn 'Onward Christian Soldiers' but while vicar of Thursley, last century, he took the story of the Sailor's Stone in the churchyard and created a Romantic novel called 'The Broomsquire'. Bridge the stream at the bottom and follow the steep path up out of this deep combe.

Follow the path out of the woods, beside Ridgeway Farm and onto the surfaced road. A glance back gives a good view of the Tudor farmhouse.

Continue along the surfaced lane to the junction ahead with Hyde Lane and continue ahead again, signposted Upper Ridgeway Farm (a short cut can be achieved by turning right down Sailors Lane). The farm is soon reached on a bend round the duck pond and what an attractive Tudor grouping this all makes; just the subject for a Helen Allingham watercolour. She lived a little to the east at Sandhills and worked in this area regularly.

Turn right just before the first bend after the duck pond to take a track down through the trees. Fork right at the field entrance to take the footpath down the gully (can be wet in winter).

Turn right at the road and proceed past yet another Tudor farm. The ramble now follows the road for just over ½ mile through countryside thick with a rich variety of trees. Soon after the farm there are hornbeams on the left – look for hawfinches feeding on the fruits in the autumn. Although uncommon they have been recorded through here. There is such a rich mixture of coniferous and broadleaved trees that many species of birds come to feed and shelter.

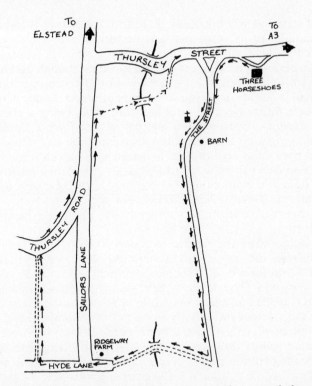

Ignore the turning right up Sailors Lane; sailors used these tracks across the heathland when trudging the London to Portsmouth route and so did the cattle and sheep drovers so some are also called the Drovers' Track etc.

Turn right onto a signposted footpath after ½ mile. It's rather concealed in the trees but is just before the 'slow' painted on the road.

Follow the path through the heathland woods and bridge the stream to continue down to a low stile that puts you into a clearing rank with waterside vegetation.

Bridge the stream ahead and continue to the stile.

Cross the stile and turn left along a driveway to another attractive group of cottages on the roadside.

Turn right and follow the lane up round the bend. This isn't very safe for ramblers so after the first bend cut off up the path up the right hand bank. Here the remnants of the heath persist – cross-leaved heath, golden rod etc.

Turn right when back on the lane again and follow it along to the Three Horseshoes.

Farnham
The Wheatsheaf

No wonder this pub is popular; you can step inside any day and get a range of hot rolls from the carvery, quick and without fuss. These are their house specialities and just what ramblers appreciate if it's a chilly day. The pub does offer an alternative menu if preferred and all of it is home-made. As for drink specialities, the lovers of Real Ale will find a choice between Webster's and Ruddles County.

There is no separate restaurant but groups are still welcome. If the organiser phones in advance places will be reserved. There is no garden as such but a patio at the rear which has six tables taking six persons each. Children and dogs are usually accepted.

Opening hours: Monday-Saturday 11 am-11 pm; Sunday 12 noon-3 pm; 7 pm-10.30 pm. Food served 12 noon-2 pm seven days a week. Bar snacks are available in the evenings.

Telephone: 0252 725132.

How to get there: The Wheatsheaf is in West Street. Leave the central car park by the main entrance, turn right and follow Downing Street to the top and turn left out along West Street. On the left the Job Centre soon comes into view, partly obscuring The Wheatsheaf beyond.

Length of the walk: 2 ¼ miles. O.S. Map Landranger Series 186.

This ancient castle town, which has some of the finest Georgian architecture in England and beautiful countryside all around, is well worth a visit. It is unspoiled by all the development of Aldershot and Farnborough that puts such a blot on the map by its side.

There are so many rewarding routes and villages to explore around here. Hundreds of people come to the town itself to explore its past, visit the castle, see exhibitions at the Maltings or to go to the theatre so the ramble chosen is a stroll round some of the town attractions.

The Walk

Turn right out of the pub and right again down an alley that leads into the top corner of the churchyard. Already the town centre seems well and truly left behind as the route broadens into a wonderful space with the great medieval church in the centre, the Victorian school buildings running along the top and a tempting range of 'backs' running down the distant east side. Take time to wander around here and you'll soon see why it attracts so many artists and photographers. The table tomb by the north door of the church is William Cobbett's, the Farnham born politician and writer ('Rural Rides' etc).

Make your way over the range of old backs on the east side where you will find the Church Lanes are still surfaced with local ironstone sets (not cobbles strictly speaking). It is tempting to explore all of them but aim to finish your wandering at the bottom and proceed out along Lower Church Lane. Note the car park on the right for the route will cross that, but first look at the Georgian houses on the corner with Downing Street. There are two together of national importance, of which No.3 of 1717 with its incredible doorway carved out of brick is perhaps the most impressive.

Return to the car park previously noted and cross to the far left corner where a footway goes through to the riverside. Ahead is the Old Maltings, saved from developers with some difficulty and now converted to public use.

Cross the bridge to the Maltings and see if there is anything of interest happening today.

Continue round the building in an anticlockwise direction to reach the street and walk along to the bridge. This way gives further peeps at Farnham's 18th/19th century heritage, funded by the richness of the local soils for hops and corn. Note the pub formerly called The Jolly Farmer but now The William Cobbett to commemorate the man's birth there.

Cross the road at the bridge to enter the riverside park at the left end of the parapet and follow the riverside path through to the next street, South Street.

Cross South Street and continue along the riverside route. The formal lawns and trees now change to a more natural landscape with plenty for naturalists to look out for.

Turn right at the end, signposted Kimbers Lane and at the next junction follow the gravel path, bearing left at the fork. Turn left at the end and pass the old pump house to reach the main road. Turn left and walk the few yards up to the traffic lights where the junction needs to be crossed almost diagonally to reach the little St. James Avenue on the other side. This leads steeply up to the park.

Enter the park and turn left to follow the path right across this lowest level of the medieval park that was attached to the castle. The route is surfaced so anyone in their 'town' clothes need not worry! Here there is the option of exploring at will this wonderful stretch of grassland and trees, folded up over the hills with little streams and a richness of wildlife in the hollows. From the higher points the view left reveals the cedar trees around the castle which saves anyone getting lost as the exit is on that side to the left.

Leave the park over in that far lower corner and follow the footway down to the street and turn right along Park Row with its old buildings and peeps through to others; the castle to the right, the backs of the almshouses to the left.

Arriving in Farnham's famous Castle Street presents ramblers with a scenic site of Georgian architecture to explore. All ramblers need to know is that by crossing the street at the bottom an alley leads between the buildings to the car park. Anyone thinking of turning right and walking right up Castle Street to visit the castle at the top

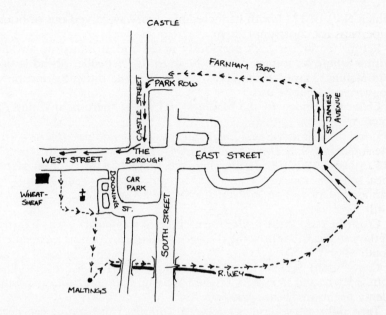

should know that it becomes very steep with a long flight of steps – seven at a time with seven paces between but they stop short of the steepest bit!

Points of Interest

The castle (English Heritage) is Norman, built for the Bishop of Winchester, and unusual for having the curtain wall around the bottom of the mound instead of the top. The keep tower has gone but there is still some interest (guided tours on tape) and expansive views. The domestic buildings are still in use, with guided tours on Wednesday afternoons.

The church is one of the largest medieval churches in Surrey, reflecting the prosperity of the town at that time as a centre of the wool trade. The castle gave it prominence too as it was the home of the Bishops of Winchester – the diocese that provided more great men of State than any other. Inside the church there is a great sense of space and light but not a great deal of interest. It does contain some of the medieval wooden screens, important in Surrey which has few, but don't expect anything as wonderful as the screens in the West Country or East Anglia!

Thorpe Green
The Rose and Crown

The Rose and Crown (Courage) is an attractive old pub, set back from the road, beside the green in just the way people imagine. Inside, it has the same 'village pub' image, created and guarded by the landlord, Mr. Duff-Cole, a Londoner who always wanted a good old English pub, out 'in the sticks', with his locals sitting round the fire in winter – yes, a real fire. Long may his successors keep it that way!

In summer though, this pub's image changes dramatically. As soon as the sun shines it becomes a family pub, but only adults are allowed into the bar. For the children there is the green and a garden, with a bouncy castle! (Saturdays 12 noon-6 pm and Sunday lunchtimes.)

Meals are served every lunchtime and evening meals are served Monday to Friday. It's good food, appreciated by the regulars: mostly traditional menus but with one or two surprises. Opening hours: 12 noon-3 pm; 5 pm-11 pm (7 pm-10.30 pm Sunday). (Open all day Saturday.)

Telephone: 0344 842338.

How to get there: Out over Staines Bridge southwards, through Egham Hythe on the B3376, left onto the B388 for Thorpe and then right onto the B389 brings you to Thorpe Green. There isn't a village to explore, just one of the largest village greens in England.

Length of the walk: 3 miles. O.S. Map Landranger Series 176.

At Thorpe Green there's plenty of room for children and dogs to let off steam, with sports areas, a playground and natural areas of grass and trees, plus a terrific sense of wide open space (especially when it's windy!). It is an ideal lunch place for anyone planning an afternoon in the area, whether a walk by Virginia Water lake and totem pole or round the Savill Garden or taking the children to the amusements at Thorpe Park.

This exhilarating ramble is by trackway and field paths out through the countryside towards Prune Hill and back through Stroude — a village built to serve the Holloway Sanatorium.

The Walk

On leaving the pub turn left and walk up the lane running alongside the green. At the fork bear right and head for the tennis courts on the edge of the green. Young oak trees are growing up on the right while at the corner is a mature one that has been there about 200 years.

Bear left to follow the path between white posts, through the trees and into the shade. Stay on this lane until it reaches the main road. On the way, notice 'Tudor House' with its black timber framing and white infill panels. Sharp eyes will find also a thatched cottage and spot in the front garden next door an old two-wheeled cart. There are some modern intrusions along here too but they have given rise to some less than common weeds for the wild flower enthusiasts. Soon the main road is reached.

Turn right at the main road, then cross it, heading for the brick chimneys of Great Fosters ahead. A glance over your shoulder will reveal the tower of the Holloway Sanatorium up on the hill.

Turn left after about 100 yards, onto a footpath signposted to Prune Hill. The route is clear but overhung with grasses and trees, giving occasional views out right to Great Fosters. Pass a shady pool, with yellow irises in June, and the edge of a meadow is reached.

Cross two stiles and follow the path worn into the turf across this open field. It is a traditional meadow full of wild flowers that have been exterminated elsewhere. There's a long list of wild grasses and the damp soil supports old favourites like the pink ragged robins and not all the buttercups are the common ones. Take care to keep to the path and not harm this heritage.

Take a moment to look upwards too, so as not to miss the building up on the hill. It is the Royal Holloway College, of national architectural importance.

Cross the stile and follow the path past the cottage.

Cross the stile and turn left along the track road. The royal history of the district shows itself a little as Crown Cottages are passed on the left and a little further along, on the right, two more. Notice the heraldic stone set into the wall, dated 1902, and bearing the device of King Edward VII.

Cross the stile and continue ahead on the farm track and just before you reach the old farm buildings turn left through the kissing gate and head for the Sanatorium Tower.

Cross another stile and continue along the track through the fields to the kissing gate at the end.

Follow the lane out to the main road and turn right. Notice Stroude Villas opposite with their wide flung gables, built at the turn of the century to provide homes for the Sanatorium staff. On the right is a little white building that may catch your eye; it is the old chapel.

Cross the road and turn left into 'The Lane', at the bottom join the footpath which bears round to the left.

Cross the stream and follow the lane, at the junction turn right and emerge at the large 'Tudor House'.

Follow the path back to the tennis courts, turn right and the lane will lead back to the start.

Points of Interest

Holloway Sanatorium. The views on this ramble are of the great central tower for which the architect was W.H. Crossland. It is not his design, for it is an almost exact copy of the Cloth Hall at Ypres. It was built for Thomas Holloway who had made a fortune out of Holloway's Pills; he is said to have spent a million pounds a year on mass advertising. Towards the end of his life he lavished his money on public works, being well able to send Crossland to the Continent to make detailed architectural drawings and measurements of famous buildings to recreate in England. The Sanatorium opened in 1884 and is an important example of our Victorian heritage.

Royal Holloway College. This is Thomas Holloway's companion piece to his Sanatorium and again he employed Crossland as architect. This time he sent him to France to come back with all the drawings and measurements necessary to create this scaled-down version of Chateau Chambord. It was built, beginning 1879, as a college for women – a quite extraordinary idea to the male-dominated society of the day, with only Girton College (1869) to pave the way in England, although the United States had examples.

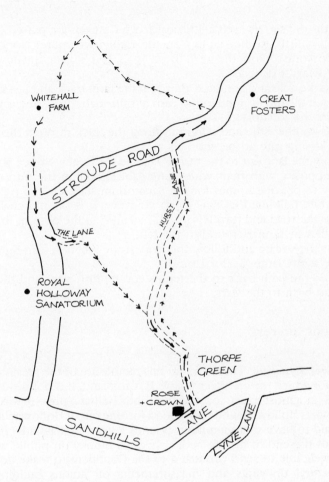

Stroude School and Church. This intriguing grouping in the street of Stroude began with the farmhouse of 1648 at the left hand end, which was the only house here. Then in the early 1800s the local population was sufficient to need a church and a school. The farmhouse was extended to the right to provide a dual purpose room. The connecting door still has peepholes through which the teacher kept an eye on the children. Later, the vestry extension was added at right angles out the back and there one of the windows has two quarries of clear glass so that the cleric could peep down the road towards Great Fosters to see if his congregation was coming.

Shere
The Prince of Wales

'By Shere standards the pub is practically modern' laughed the landlord, 'It's only about 150 years old'. Inside there is a good atmosphere, the usual range of Young's beers which find much favour hereabouts and a popular menu with the house specials changing daily. All the meals are homemade except for items like sausage which are bought in, but the pies have never seen a factory wrapper. They attract rambling groups as much as the village does and here the Prince of Wales is lucky enough to have an extra outside Functions/Children's Room where rambling groups often choose to go to have their meal together. It can accommodate up to 30 but remember Shere can be a busy place so any large groups needing meals are politely requested to phone through an advance warning before the day. Otherwise there is no separate restaurant.

Opening hours: Monday-Saturday 11 am-2.30 pm; 6 pm-11 pm. Sunday 12 noon-3 pm; 7 pm-10.30 pm. Food served: Monday-Sunday 12 noon-2 pm; Wednesday, Thursday, Friday and Saturday 7.30 pm-9.30 pm. Telephone: 0483 202313.

How to get there: Shere lies just off the A25 between Guildford and Dorking. The Prince of Wales is up the street beyond the central triangle. Motorists who decide they must get as close as possible will find limited parking in front of the pub and a large car park behind.

Parking: Parking can be a major problem. Save yourself the bother and leave the car on the edge; there's a small car park hidden on the left off the approach road from Guildford (Upper Street), or, coming from Dorking, there is street parking along the approach road off the by-pass (Gomshall Lane). Either place leaves only a short walk to the tiny village centre.

Length of the walk: 1¼ miles. O.S. Map Landranger Series 187.

The fascination of Shere lies in its small scale closeness. From the old wellhead set in the wall, Middle Street soon crosses the low arched bridge over the little river Tillingbourne where white ducks bounce along or sunbathe on the bank under the weeping willow. Then there's the tiniest of village centres, a triangle with cottages on two sides closing in on the lychgate and the most beautiful of Surrey's Gothic churches.

Visited by thousands and deemed by so many to be the prettiest village in Surrey, Shere needs no introduction to Surrey folk. If on the other hand you come as a visitor then this is one of the places that everyone tells you not to miss. It is ideal for those who want a trip out but with someone who doesn't want to walk very far; much of the centre can be enjoyed from a wheelchair, and there is wheelchair access to the pub from the rear car park.

The Walk

Take care leaving the pub as you step out onto the narrow hill. Cross over to walk along Spinning Walk – a reminder of the days when Shere was an important centre of the local woollen industry, specialising here in a mixed weave of wool and linen called fustian.

Turn left at the end, down Church Hill, to get a good view of the south side of the church. Much of it is built from stone dug out of the ground only a short distance away and by special agreement with the authorities this quarry was reworked to provide modern restoration stones. The rarity to spot is the outside staircase at the west end of the church.

Stop and take note of options. Obviously there is the church to visit opposite. On Saturday and Sunday afternoons from April to September it is worth turning right and entering the private drive to visit the farm for its museum, demonstrations etc. Note also that from the back right hand corner of the churchyard there is a footpath

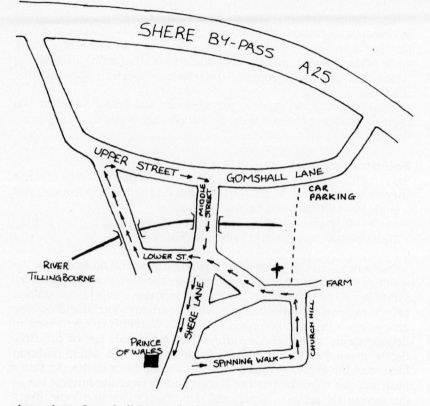

through to Gomshall Lane which may be convenient for returning to the car. Looking left reveals the village centre.

Enter the church by the west door. There is a guide book available and also other guides to the village and district including more rambles. There is much to enjoy from brasses to old musical instruments.

Proceed ahead on leaving the church, out under the lychgate and so into the village centre, keeping to the right to cross over to the riverbank.

Continue along the riverside and so out along Lower Street, enjoying the old houses and cottage garden flowers. Don't turn back, like so many do, but continue to the junction at the end and bear right over the Tillingbourne at the old ford.

Continue up the hill. The rural setting can be appreciated more from this side and even on busy days this can be quieter. Some people will find it steep too.

Turn right at the top. This may well have been the road by which you arrived so this is a chance to see it at more leisure, from the wild flowers in the bank to the old manor's overhead footbridge. Note some of the timber-framed houses infilled with flint rather than plaster panels (most unusual). Some of the framing is of elm rather than the usual oak.

The car park is on the left; the wellhead and village street on the right; walk straight ahead along Gomshall Lane if the car was parked there.

Points of Interest
Several little guide books are available in the village (try the church if shops shut) for more walks, information on the historic houses, and a guide to the Hurtwood behind the village.

Shere Museum is up by the Prince of Wales.

The Church – in particular note the stained glass and memorials in the south east chapel. The medieval glass in the east window includes symbols of the Evangelists and is of superior quality; the golden brown eagle of St. John being especially striking. The shield of blue and yellow chequers belonged to the de Warenne family, based in Reigate Castle and Earls of Surrey. The memorials are of the Bray family, given this manor after the Battle of Bosworth where tradition has it that Sir Reginald Bray pulled the crown from under the thorn bush and put it on the head of Henry Tudor. Here the interest lies in the memorials' rebus – a pictorial pun. The device that looks like a box with a chopping knife fixed to its side is a bray, a device used in the conversion of flax to linen. A modern replica is sometimes demonstrated at the farm museum.

West Clandon
The Bull's Head

The Bull's Head (Courage) is one of the large timber-framed Tudor farmhouses right beside the street. It became a set of cottages but has now been converted back to serve as the village pub and indeed a good 'village pub atmosphere' is maintained within.

Your hosts will serve almost any drink except a pressure bitter – only real ale here, plus a wide range of meals, English and Continental dishes. Unlike a lot of Surrey inns, meals are served here in the evenings (except Sundays) as well as at midday, despite not having a separate restaurant. Also good news for ramblers is the size of the meal. If you need to fuel a good walk then this is the place to come and all for a very modest price too.

The Bull's Head keeps its Tudor atmosphere with its close spaces on different levels and original great oak beams, unspoilt by modernity. There is parking for about 30 cars.

Opening hours: 11 am-2.30 pm (3 pm Saturday and Sunday), 5.30 pm-11 pm (10.30 pm Sunday).

Telephone: 0483 222444.

How to get there: West Clandon is beside the A246 Guildford to Leatherhead road, in a rural setting free from traffic noise. Within easy reach are such beauty spots as Newlands Corner and the Silent Pool, and the National Trust houses of Hatchlands, Polesden Lacey, and Clandon Park in the village itself.

Length of the walk: 4 miles. O.S. Map Landranger Series 186.

The village is strung along 'The Street' which runs beside the Park from the main road out into the countryside to the north. It doesn't have a focal point, just an ever-changing succession of attractive buildings, ranging from the Norman and medieval church to the timber-framed houses of Tudor times and then the later cottages in brick and tile, all nestling comfortably between trees and gardens.

This attractive ramble leads you through some of the beautiful local countryside, which often goes unnoticed because it can be obscured from the roads by trees. It is all that people imagine the countryside to be – a gentle landscape of fields and trees with streams and lakes. The difference is that this particular setting has not been created entirely by generations of farmers but by the vision of one man – Capability Brown, working to create a 'natural' landscape in the Clandon Park acres for the Onslow family.

The Walk

From the Bull's Head turn left along the path which begins to rise attractively above the road and as it moves away from it start looking for White Lodge, on the left, and the public footpath sign pointing off up the side of the drive. Follow that and when the drive bears left the path continues ahead, plunging into trees and countryside.

At the next driveway cross over and cross the stile to continue along the grassy path down into the valley. Pass between high banks to a stile at the bottom and continue, but look right to enjoy views of the lake.

Continue, ignoring all the side turnings, to arrive at a bridge by a ford where the track dips through the water at your side.

Follow the path to a track and so to a fork, at which bear right beside a landscape of open fields with trees on the left through which there are peeps over the hill to farm buildings. The highest point is soon reached with the land falling away in every direction.

Where the track meets another, continue ahead along a path overhung with trees that goes down into the lowlands, and at the fork bear left to climb again, over a ridge and into the trees. Follow the path ahead through the thick woodland to the road and there turn left and follow it. It will pass a variety of housing, including Tanglewood which was formerly two cottages from the 16th and 17th centuries

(Grade II listed). Look out for Thrift Vale on the right and take the path opposite, slightly worn, through the trees. This cuts down to another road so beware of letting children and dogs run on ahead.

Cross the road and up the bank and turn left, to approach the old part of Merrow and interesting chimneys soon come into view. Cottages on the right dated 1900 are already mellowed and looking old while the brick and flint garden walls give local character. The majority of the housing, however, along this short stretch, is modern but not entirely without interest. Mayrecroft on the right gains character from its style of brickwork and dark wood. Looking ahead there are more solid flint garden walls that are such a distinctive and beautiful characteristic of these downland villages.

At the junction, cross the road and skirt the railings to enter Merrow Street – the old village street (prior to the development along the Epsom Road). It gives the appearance of a typical country lane, with trees and hedges for cool greenery and a variety of village homes dotted along it. There's timber-framing and tile-hanging from the 16th and 17th centuries and good Georgian red brick from the 18th century and pleasing Victorian villas too.

At the end of the road turn left, walk down towards the round-about, spot the gates to Clandon Park. Take the path beside the left hand lodge, following it round the lodge and garden to the driveway and turn left to follow it. A variety of broadleaved trees shield the park landscape from the busy Epsom Road and so it's possible to enjoy immediately the great open grasslands enriched with trees spreading as far as can be seen. Ahead and to the right Clandon House can be seen in the distance, partly hidden by encircling tall trees.

Look out for a public footpath sign sending you to the left. The ground now rises giving even better views out over the parkland and from the crest, views right, over cow-dotted fields, to one of the farms, shielded by trees. With the ground still rising in that direction, Clandon House can be seen overlooking its park. The path continues downhill, however, through long grass to a line of trees which soon opens out to give more views out over pastures and paddocks.

At the track, cross over it to the right and seek the continuation of the path. This passes the farm and goes downhill to a stile with one of the farm cottages over on the right.

Cross the stile and continue to the farm track, cross it and continue ahead over the field and head for the stile that comes into view. Having crossed that you are beside woodland in a rather overgrown pathway (in summer) but are soon rewarded with close views of the lake and its swans with the path bridged across one end of it – a quiet

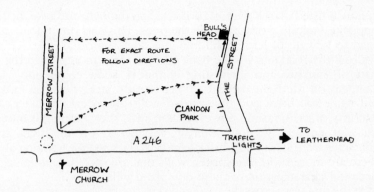

place to loiter, to hang over the parapet and spot the fish below the surface.

Follow the path which soon bridges a stream and widens to pass through tall trees on either side. More good views of parkland and house coming up.

Continue ahead (without turning left or right at the crossroads) until the public road is reached (the street of West Clandon). Turn left to return to the Bull's Head, passing a good variety of old buildings, some listed for preservation, or, turn right to visit Clandon Park and the medieval church.

Points of Interest

The Park: The Elizabethan House at Clandon Park was purchased by Sir Richard Onslow in 1641, it was then rebuilt c1731 by his great-grandson Thomas Onslow. The new house was designed by Giacomo Leoni and paid for by Elizabeth Knight, the wife of Thomas and one of the richest heiresses of her day.

Clandon Park, now owned by the National Trust, houses some grand collections including much that relates to the Onslow family. Also within the building is the military museum of Surrey's Infantry Regiments, displaying information and artifacts from seven regiments, dating from 1661 up to the present day.

The church. The medieval church of St. Peter and St. Paul in West Clandon has nearly all been rebuilt but do not fear, it is still worth a visit if only to look at the south wall. Here has been preserved a medieval sundial, although the gnomon has gone. It is not the usual scratch dial to show the times of the services as found in so many other churches. This is much more complicated.

Windlesham
The Half Moon

The Half Moon is a very welcoming and comfortable freehouse, with beams, open fire and part stone-flagged floor. It is set at the edge of this picturesque village, looking up to the church and old houses crowning the hill. The lunch menu is extensive, as is the range of beer, and there is a separate eating area. Children are not allowed in the bar but they are welcome in the large beer garden, which has a children's play area with a Wendy house and a boot!

Opening hours: Monday to Thursday 11 am-2.30 pm, 5 pm-11 pm; Friday 11 am-3 pm, 5 pm-11 pm; all day Saturday; Sunday 12 pm-3 pm, 7 pm-11 pm. Food served every day 12 noon-2 pm (2.30 pm on Sundays). There are no evening meals.

Telephone: 0276 473329.

How to get there: Windlesham lies on the east side of the A30, just north of Bagshot.

44

Parking: There is a lay-by outside the church where cars may be parked.

Length of the walk: 3½ miles. O.S. Map Landranger Series 186.

Windlesham is far older than it looks at first sight. The medieval church was struck by lightning and burnt down in 1676, but many old cottages and farms survive from those early days as Windlesham is on the better soils at the edge of the arid heathlands of west Surrey. Nearby Bagshot Park has given the area a royal history and many paths cut out across farmland and parkland through this little-known corner of Surrey.

The Walk

Turn left out of the Half Moon and first left into New Road. Go immediately left again onto the bridleway. Fork right onto the footpath and cross the stile into the fields.

Cross the open field heading for the willow tree. Turn left and follow the path to the next corner, cross the stile and turn right along the bridleway heading for the M3. Keep on this track to go up and over the motorway footbridge.

At the cross tracks on the other side carry on ahead through the gate and follow the path through the woodland. The route emerges into grassland with many newly planted trees through which a broad swathe of grass leads ahead and downhill to a gated entrance and path junction. Here turn left and follow the path into the landscaped grounds that have been showing up on your left. Now the route runs along beside the chain of lakes.

Go through the gate at the end and follow the lane past the houses, through the large gates and head out along the lane. (Don't turn left.)

Turn left at the highway and take the first right into Hook Mill Lane. Walk along this quiet lane up the hill and down through the trees on the other side until you reach the first track on the left ('Public Bridleway'). Follow this all the way, sometimes beside a stream but always through old oak and hazel woodland.

Keep straight ahead at the junctions to cross the M3 once more, and follow the lane out to the highway. Turn left on reaching the road and follow it into the newer part of the village. Keep on this road as it goes downhill and keep bearing left as it runs into Thorndown Lane.

Soon, on the right, there is a long range of rest-home bungalows; turn right onto the footpath immediately after them. Here the fields have now been built on but the footpath still goes straight through, crossing over any residential roads, to the main highway beyond.

Turn right for a few yards along this highway and then left onto a

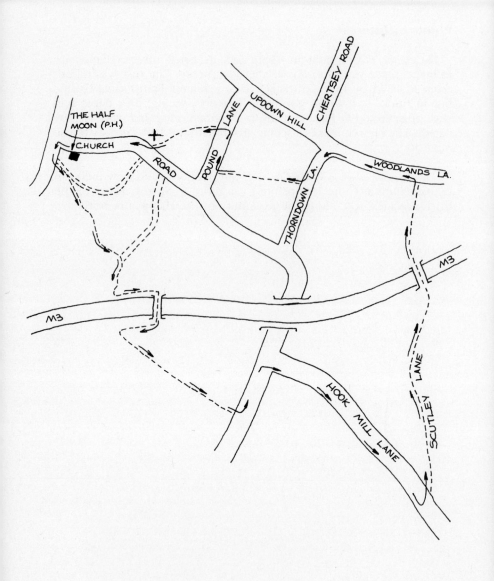

footpath at the speed limit sign. This path goes up to the church. Turn right outside and the Half Moon is at the bottom of the hill.

Points of Interest

The church was rebuilt in 1680, and its brick tower (Hampshire influence) and south porch are the best pieces. The rest was rebuilt again in 1874 by Ewan Christian. He re-created Transitional Gothic but in brick – it looks good and is worth seeing. The choir stall was presented by Elizabeth II to commemorate her stay in the parish. The church makes a scenic group with the 18th century house next door.

The thatched cottage in Pound Lane (left out of church and downhill) can be described as 'pure Hampshire' – a rarity in Surrey. Many of the brick cottages, too, show the proximity of the Hampshire border.

East Molesey
The Bell

The Bell is away from the tourist pubs around Hampton Court Bridge, being set well back from the Thames by the banks of the lesser known river Ember, down beyond the church. It's quiet down there, with free street parking if the pub's park is full. The black beams and white plaster of this late medieval building, here before the palace was built, are most inviting but don't miss the unusual rooftop weathervane before you enter. There's the usual range of drinks with a good variety on the menu. Food is home-made with two or three house specials to choose from and these change from day to day. There is no separate restaurant but the pub will cater for group bookings. Everyone is welcome and there is a large garden.

Opening hours: Monday-Saturday 11 am-11 pm, Sunday 12 noon-3 pm; 7 pm-10.30 pm. Food served Monday to Friday 12 noon-9.30 pm; Saturday 12 noon-5.30 pm; Sunday 12 noon-2 pm.

Telephone: 081 941 0400.

How to get there: East Molesey is situated on the Surrey bank of the Thames, across the bridge from Hampton Court Palace on the A309 Esher road.

Length of the walk: Altogether 3¼ miles but there is a shorter option of 1¼ miles. O.S. Map Landranger Series 176.

East Molesey is a surprise. A maze of narrow streets where Tudor nudges Georgian next to grand early 19th century amidst a jostle of later little buildings, all creating a sense of place. The older buildings are down by The Bell with the Old Manor House and Quillets Royal, dated 1530, catching the eye right on the side of the lane.

The first part of this fascinating ramble is a short (1¼ mile) exploration down by the rivers Mole and Ember. Then there is a second option linking the pub with the palace bridge area via the historic riverside grassland of Molesey Hurst (about 2 miles). They will probably seem longer due to the urban setting and depending where ramblers explore any by-ways.

The Walk

To the Ember and the Mole: Turn right out of the pub but as you do so notice the long terrace opposite showing how well old housing can be refurbished to give modern homes of character without being pretentious. Doesn't reinstating stone paving slabs for the pavement make all the difference when viewed along their length?

Proceed to the end but do not swing round to the right. Instead approach the end house to find the bridleway on the left before its entrance. The house, Green Arden, is early 18th century of local importance architecturally.

Turn left down the bridleway. It can be wet in winter if you have your 'palace' shoes on (!) but it's great to get off the hard surfaces and enjoy a bit of mud and wet grass!

Beware of letting young children run ahead as the open riverbank is just round the corner.

The river Mole is quite a surprise – slow and deep and quiet. It started near Gatwick Airport, looked up at Box Hill, missed Dorking, came through Leatherhead and round behind Esher to here. In winter especially, when the Thames is cold and choppy, the waterfowl can be found here (a lot of tufted duck on the day this route was checked). With so many mature gardens and fine trees the area is always rich in birdlife.

Bear right with the path and follow the bank. Two bridges are in sight with a weir beyond. Turn left over the first bridge and follow the path ahead.

Cross the next bridge over another river. This time it is the little river Ember. Just after Esher the Mole forks and this is the right fork and will rejoin the Mole just before entering the Thames below Hampton Court Bridge.

Follow the path through the buildings (weir on right), reminding us this was all farmland once. Over on the right is the historic site of Ember or Imber Court where a number of notable people have lived (eg the Onslows; see West Clandon ramble) and which is now used by the police service.

Proceed ahead along the suburban street but look for a footpath off to the left through the fence.

Turn left down the footpath and follow the road to its end. A few good plants to look out for in the mature gardens. The road ahead can be busy so mind children.

Turn left and cross over as the bridge ahead has pavement on one side only.

After the bridge cross back and bear round to the left to enter the quieter Walton Road, which becomes East Molesey's shopping street, and already there is great variety in the buildings.

Take the first left into Matham Road, which leaves the street behind to go round in a loop back onto Walton Road, so there is the option of ignoring this turning and taking the second left to shorten the route.

The only reason to take Matham Road is to leave the street as soon as possible and because many ramblers enjoy looking at the big old houses. The best is Matham House right on that first corner which now has a beautiful exterior. Further round are examples of revival Dutch gables (1885 etc). Matham Road joins with St. Mary's Road just before Walton Road and so turn into St. Mary's Road. The parish church was renewed in 1864-7 and by golly doesn't it look it – but – go inside and you'll find it light and airy and spacious.

Continue down the road back to The Bell.

To Molesey Hurst and the Palace: Turn right out of The Bell and follow the road to the end. Turn right to follow Spencer Road up to the main street and cross over into Manor Road.

Follow Manor Road to the end where it turns left and after that take the first right into Church Road and follow that to the far end beyond the church, which is in a central island. This is Kent Town.

Cross the main Molesey Hurst Road running parallel to the Thames at the northern far end of Church Road. Opposite is Graburn Way with some peculiar gates and a wide expanse of rough grassland on which dogs and children can let off steam. Although largely forgotten now, this is one of the most significant fields in English sporting history.

Turn right and walk down the Hurst to Hampton Court Bridge; designed by Sir Edwin Lutyens in the Wren style of the Palace. Cross

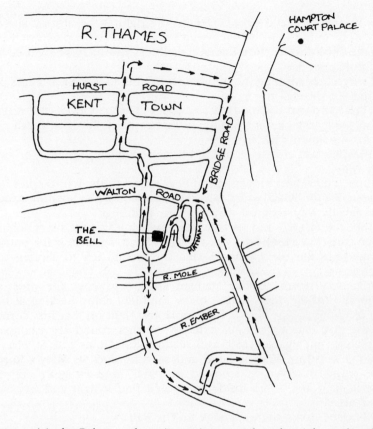

over to visit the Palace, otherwise swing round to the right and walk down Bridge Road skirting the eastern end of Kent Town.

Turn right into Walton Road and the route back to The Bell is now the same as in the first section of ramble with St. Mary's Road second left.

Points of Interest

Graburn Way Gates used to close the roadway when this was part of Molesey's Hurst Park horse racing course. The sport had begun here by at least 1737 but the Jockey Club closed the course in 1887 as unsafe. Improvements led to its reopening and the course was closed finally on 10th October 1962. In the earlier phases it was known as Hampton Races and very popular they were too; read Dickens' version in 'Nicholas Nickleby'.

51

Shepperton
The King's Head

The pub is one of the homely buildings on the lower side of Shepperton from where you step into a suitably old and wooden interior: varnished wooden floor, panelled walls, original oak beams, wooden seating and of course an open fire. No wonder tradition has it that notables such as King Charles II and Nelson came here with their mistresses; both unsubstantiated but enough to give the pub its name.

A separate 'Cabin Bar' acts as the restaurant and group bookings are welcome but if large then of course prior notice needs to be given. A range of beers is available: Courage, Wadsworth's 6X, Marstons Pedigree etc.

Opening hours: Monday-Friday 11 am-3 pm; 5.30 pm-11 pm; Saturday all day. Sunday 12 noon-3 pm; 7 pm-10.30 pm. Food served: Monday-Friday 12 noon-2.15 pm; 7 pm-10 pm. Saturday 12 noon-2.15 pm; 7 pm-10 pm. Not Sundays.

Telephone: 0932 221910.

How to get there: The King's Head with its little walled garden, is right in the little Church Square, signposted off the by-pass, with parking outside in the Square if you are lucky but when this is full follow the signs for the larger car park a few hundred yards along the street towards modern Shepperton.

52

Length of the walk: 3¼ miles. O.S. Map Landranger Series 176.

There can't be many places in south east England where a country ramble includes a ferry crossing over the river but then Surrey is full of surprises. Both Shepperton and Weybridge retain much of their old charm and interest despite all the pressures of being so close to London and the novelty of the river crossing will help make a visit memorable. Should your visit not coincide with ferry times there is the option of driving round to Weybridge and starting the ramble on that side of the river.

The Walk

Turn right out of the pub and follow the buildings along the alley out of the square and you'll arrive in another one, even smaller than the first. Here the Thames sweeps round in a great loop to wash against the roadway, probably jostling with hungry ducks. If not, start throwing a few pieces of bread into the water and ducks suddenly fly in from nowhere. Beyond the river are great meadows – such a contrast to what was expected.

Retrace your steps to leave Ferry Square but turn into the churchyard. The church is worth a visit.

Return to Church Square after visiting the church and enjoy the tiny townscape, known to such writers as Erasmus, George Meredith and George Eliot (the 'Shepperton' in her writings is a different village).

Look right up the street out of the square for further good views but it is hardly worth exploring as you can see the best already. Turn left out of the Square, noting the old smithy on the corner, and begin following the main road (much improved since the opening of the by-pass).

Take the first left down Ferry Lane, leaving the main road for a narrower route down to the river. Still keep an eye on children and dogs as the riverside ahead can be a bustling place at weekends. It's an enjoyable bustle though, as boaters and everyone else enjoy the river above the weir, by the Pharoah's and D'Oyly Carte Islands.

The ferry has been reinstated, so go for a crossing as in days of old. During weekdays it runs hourly on the hour (half hourly during the early morning and teatime rush); at weekends and Bank Holidays it is half hourly. Note: it ends at 5.30 pm so don't get stranded on the other side! Fares 50p single, 80p return.

Arriving at Weybridge don't go off to the left but walk ahead up Thames Street. Again this can be a busy corner so take care. Note the entrance to the Wey Navigation off the Thames; one of England's earliest inland waterways (opened 1653) and leading to the southernmost point of the network.

On the left is the Lincoln Arms, built 1700 and barely changed

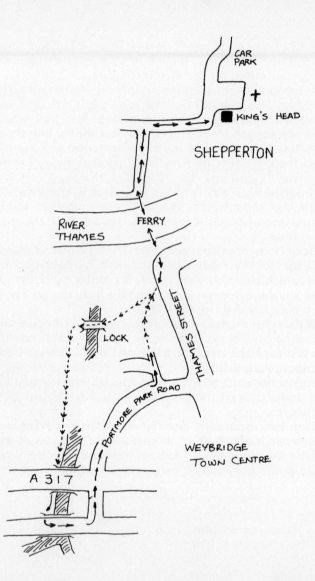

externally although the inside has been modernised. It has always been a pub, serving the former river traffic, brewing its own beer and housing the wharf master. It was part of the Oatlands estates owned by the Earls of Lincoln, hence the pub name.

On the right the riverside used to be the royal wharves, back in Tudor times, when the Royal Palace of Oatlands owned all the land.

Thus the name of the next pub is no surprise but here turn right down the footpath and at the junction turn right again to follow through to the Lock Cottage on the Wey Navigation.

At the lock, the lock keeper's cottage is one of a set surviving on the waterway although this one was rebuilt in 1976, retaining its former appearance. Downstream is a rare single-gate lock which raises the level just enough for laden craft to clear the cill into the main pound lock. It is claimed that pound locks were introduced into this country from the Continent by Sir Richard Weston who masterminded this waterway – and you can argue about that for a very long time.

Cross the waterway (which is both river Wey and canal in one here) and follow the towpath. This travels through trees and countryside; a great surprise considering it is parallel with the main street of Weybridge.

A pool between two road bridges is reached which was formerly the wharfage for Weybridge. On the corner is preserved a vertical roller post which guided towing ropes, for at this point the canal cuts off right while the river pours in under the main bridge. The two courses have been divided since Ripley.

Walkers have to take the footbridge up on to the road and there turn left, although it is worth deviating to explore this corner. Turn left at the first road and cross the main road ahead into the continuation of Portmore Park Road.

Follow this road, which is late Victorian development in the Garden City style, built in the grounds of the former park of the Earls of Portmore.

Turn left, eventually, into the top of Radnor Road and then keep right into Church Walk – another unexpected corner of Weybridge. Follow this through to Thames Street and turn left to retrace your route to the ferry and so back to Shepperton.

Epsom Downs
The Rubbing House

The Rubbing House is, literally, right on the edge of the Derby racecourse, so obviously this is a pub for the casual rambler to avoid on race meeting days and during Derby Week (the first week in June). At other times it is a good pub at a famous spot on top of the downs, where views can be enjoyed without going further than the patio. There's plenty of on-site car parking. This is not an ancient building with blackened beams to admire but it has its own individual interest. The walls are covered with the portraits of past racing champions. To top it off there is Real Ale and home-made food; they will take group bookings but there is no separate restaurant. Nevertheless children and dogs are welcome, within the limits of the law.

Opening hours: 11 am-2.30 pm; 5.30 pm-11 pm Monday-Saturday, 12 noon-3 pm; 7 pm-10.30 pm Sunday. Food served: 12 noon-2 pm, in the summer when there is greater demand (say Easter to October) food is served 6 pm-9 pm on Wednesday to Saturday evenings inclusive.

Telephone: 0372 723245.

How to get there: Epsom is a busy modern town where they have recently changed the road system to try and improve the flow of traffic through the High Street. Turn off the B290 Epsom road (Downs Road) at the traffic lights below the grandstand, on to Langley Vale Road which takes you by underpass under the racetrack, and then take the first left to spiral up the access road to the pub. Beware, the road system beside the grandstand has been simplified and may not be quite the same as your map suggests.

Length of the walk: 3 miles. O.S. Map Landranger Series 187.

Little remains to remind visitors that this was once an important spa town; the first in England to have permanent buildings, after the mineral waters charged with 'Epsom Salts' were discovered in 1618. Today the best part of Epsom is up on the Downs and the pub has been chosen with that in mind, right next to the famous racecourse and adjacent to the best vantage point for grand views.

This exhilarating ramble takes you over the Downs and parts of the racecourse itself so will not be possible during meetings. At other times the Downs are a wonderful wide open space flung over the hills, that can make you feel on top of the world. It is also a working landscape so keep clear of horses in training, especially if you have dogs and little children with you.

The Walk

Start in the car park where you get good views out over the Downs and the track and walk away from the pub, crossing its access road, out onto the grass. Look for a map display of the course area which is positioned by the roadside and use the path to the right of it to continue down over the grassland.

Cross the dirt track and continue following the clear but narrow path uphill to the racecourse.

Cross the surfaced road and cross the racetrack onto what now becomes a dirt track. The starting point for the Derby is to your right. Continue along the dirt track. The landscape of shortish grass now changes to one with longer grass etc and thus there is a different range of wildlife, especially with the butterflies in summer feeding on the downland flora.

Cross a training track through positions provided and continue downhill towards woodland (further change of wildlife), and soon the route will start ascending the Downs again. The woods stop on the hilltop and the route continues over the crest and down through open pasture.

Turn left at the bottom of the field to follow a sandy track. Just follow this round its anti-clockwise curve until eventually it reaches

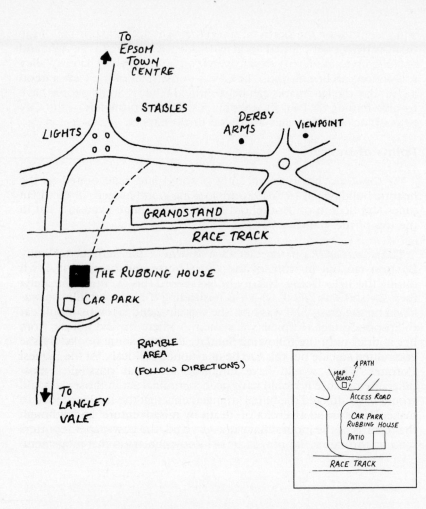

the public road (Epsom Lane North).

Turn left and use the pavement on the other side for a short distance until it is possible to cross back onto a more pleasant wide grassy verge with wide sweeping views of the course.

Continue following the grassy way back round towards the Grandstand. This is the famous Tattenham Corner where the suffragette was injured. Passing behind the Grandstand, you'll see a surfaced path that leads directly back to the pub patio.

Before following that, ramblers may prefer to cross over the road and greens to see the Derby Arms on the right with the portrait of the first Derby winner painted upon its facade. By turning to the right and walking up to the lay-by expansive views out over the Thames Valley to London can be enjoyed. The City is to the right of the view and on a clear day the landmarks can be identified readily. Some people have trouble finding St. Paul's Cathedral; it's further to the left of the City tower blocks and smaller, than you might expect.

Points of Interest

The Grandstand has been recently restored and redecorated so the historic buildings of 1914/1926 are looking grand indeed. In Victorian times Mrs Beeton of 'Household Management' fame lived in a flat in the top of the grandstand.

Tattenham Corner on the racetrack is where the suffragette Emily Davison ran out in front of the king's horse and brought it down during the 1913 Derby. History books record this event inaccurately; they say she was killed, which is misleading if readers think she was killed on the grass. She was not. She was alive and taken by motor car to Epsom Cottage Hospital (still standing) where she did not die from her injuries until the following Sunday. Further, some books say she committed suicide but this can be questioned seriously. At the inquest Coroner White would have enquired into that possibility most diligently because it would have been a criminal act in those days and would have affected the burial arrangements that the family needed to make. He returned a verdict of 'death by misadventure' and although the records of the inquest have not survived, the newspaper reporters who sat through it did not, as far as I know, question that judgement.

Godstone
The White Hart

The White Hart (Whitbread) is one of a group of ancient inns that make up the oldest such group in any Surrey village. Founded in the reign of Richard II (whose personal badge was a white hart), it was enlarged in Elizabethan times and proudly declares that last century it was 'honoured by frequent visits from Her Most Gracious Majesty Queen Victoria'.

This massive great timber-framed building is now part of the Beefeater chain and therefore provides restaurant meals all day Sunday, which should suit ramblers. It is not always easy to get a meal in Surrey on a Sunday. Here there are no limits to group bookings. Ramblers do not have to use the restaurant of course: there is the normal range of bar food available, with chef's specials changing daily on rotation.

Opening hours: Monday-Saturday 11 am-2.30 pm; Sunday 12 noon-3 pm. Monday-Thursday 6 pm-11 pm; Friday-Saturday 5.30 pm-11 pm; Sunday 7 pm-10.30 pm.

Telephone: 0883 742521.

How to get there: Godstone is just off the M25. It's just to the south of Junction 7 but anyone travelling in an anti-clockwise direction needs to be alert to the fact that the next junction after 8 is the motorway interchange not Junction 7. Turn off too early and it's a very long way back!

Length of the walk: 3 miles. O.S. Map Landranger Series 187.

Godstone is one of those villages where the centre moved site during the course of its history and so the rambler is guided from one to the other and back by way of the hills and valleys and ponds that go to make this a varied and rewarding district to explore.

The Walk

Follow the right hand side of the pub away from the road, signposted to Godstone church. This route leads past Bay Pond which is on the left and is maintained as a nature reserve. At quiet times it is always worth pausing here to see what wildlife is about.

Follow the route (surfaced nowadays) up the hillside through farmland, sheep and trees to Church Lane at the top. Turn right at the T-junction with Church Lane. The parish church is opposite and well worth a visit, with the almshouses beside it and a small gathering of distinctive village homes in a variety of styles, and of course the old school. This is all worth a few minutes to view.

Continue to the right down Church Lane and soon it plunges between high banks down the hillside. The lane is overarched with trees, sheltered in winter, cool in summer, and full of wild flowers. Note the Old Packhouse Cottage on the way down. Turn left at the bottom onto the A22 but only for a few yards; there's another high bank on one side and on the other a little stream from the ponds ahead.

Turn left onto footpath and bridleway clearly signposted to Tandridge. There are now two large ponds on the left but only the first is apparent at this stage. The route skirts this and turns up the bank to the left (before reaching the 'No Entry' signs), to pass between them. At this stage the second becomes visible and there is a stile on the right for anyone wishing a closer look but the route being described continues on ahead between the ponds.

(Note: since many maps were printed the Godstone by-pass has been extended down to the east of this scene. It doesn't spoil the ramble but may confuse map readers!)

Turn left when the path meets the trackway (Leigh Place on left). At the buildings the trackway bends right but then before it turns back

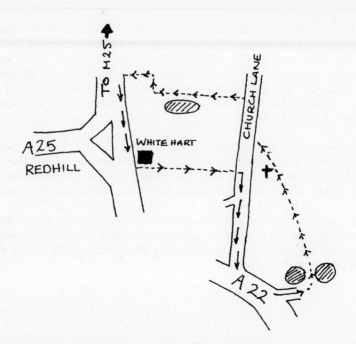

left take the signposted path off to the right. Follow it up the field. near the top of the hill take the option of bearing off to the left through the trees and shrubs into the next field. Follow the worn path diagonally downhill across the field to the trees and on the other side you will find another pond. Approach quietly for the chance of seeing herons.

Follow the path left around the pond and this will lead to the churchyard, and so out to Church Lane again.

Turn right and follow Church Lane looking for a trackway on the left, signposted for public use.

Follow the path and soon another pond comes into view which is Bay Pond again but this time from the other side. The route runs into Riders Way and across a staggered junction to reach Salisbury Road. Turn left along Salisbury Road to reach the High Street and turn left to return to the green and the White Hart.

Points of Interest

The parish church is a beautiful example of just how good a Victorianised village church can be. It is mostly due to Sir Giles Gilbert Scott, about whom this cannot always be said. He lived nearby which may have something to do with it. It's not so much his work that visitors will remember as that of some unknown sculptor in a workshop who created the wonderful capitals for Scott. They are floral, following medieval symbolism but with 19th century additions. In particular the way the spiky lilies are contrived to whirl around a capital is a masterpiece of design and on another capital you can almost smell the primroses.

The almshouses next to the church are also by Scott in the local timber-frame style but nicely mellow with golden plaster instead of harsh white. That plastering has also been pargetted in low relief like a William Morris wallpaper. The chapel inside is unbelievable for such a grand church builder as Scott. It's timbered and homely, with a fireplace, just right for almshouses but not at all the usual Scott. We can, however, see his mastery by simply standing in the lane outside and appreciating the terrific sense of presence the homes create as they range along the hilltop.

Mickleham
The Running Horses

The Running Horses is a large white walled pub with Georgian style windows of small panes and dormers in the roof: a homely place in a solid sort of way, dating back to the 16th century. The pub name was changed in 1828 from The Chequers to the Running Horses after the Derby of that year which was the only occasion on which there was a dead heat and it had to be run again on the Sunday. This time The Colonel was beaten by Cadland, as can be seen on one side of the pub sign. Unusually, the sign has a different scene on the reverse – the victorious Cadland, of which Mickleham villagers were so proud because the horse had been stabled at the pub prior to the race. It was normal practice to stable runners in neighbouring districts at Derby time and so Mickleham celebrated again in 1864 when they stabled that year's winner, Blair Athol.

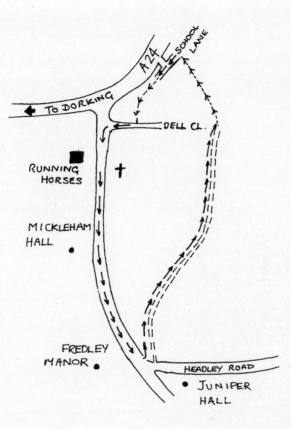

It is renowned for the quality of its food and drink and for its conference facilities in such a beautiful setting. It caters for the casual ramblers too with a range of simpler meals at sensible prices. The meal specialities change daily, and guest beers are available.

Opening hours: Monday-Saturday 11 am-11 pm; Sunday 12 noon-3 pm; 7 pm-10.30 pm. Food served: all week 12 noon-9.30 pm.

Telephone: 0372 372279.

How to get there: The Running Horses is just up the village street off the A24 Mickleham by-pass.

Length of the walk: 2½ miles. O.S. Map Landranger Series 187.

*Mickleham is easily missed as traffic roars down the busy A24 Leatherhead/
Dorking road or because visitors head for nearby Box Hill, but this quiet backwater
is well worth seeking out. It's set above the river Mole where it cuts through the
chalk hills amid famous walking country. You can explore it on foot or through the
pages of some of England's great writers from Fanny Burney and Jane Austen to
George Meredith. It attracted important French emigrees during the French
Revolution and a whole host of Victorian worthies intent on rambling through this
beautiful landscape.*

*This ramble is a simple one to follow but is not entirely easy going as it climbs
the flanks of the Downs. It's worth the effort, to enjoy this famous section of the
Mole Valley to the north of the even more famous Burford Bridge/Box Hill end. It
is all through trees so it is sheltered in winter and cool in summer. There are plenty
of opportunities to extend out onto the open Downs if ramblers wish.*

The Walk

Turn right out of the pub and follow the country lane which is also
the village street, but in days gone by was also the main London road.
The parish church is opposite and worth a visit.

The lane follows the boundary walls of Mickleham Hall for quite
some distance and climbs all the way.

Turn left at the first junction into Headley Road. Opposite this
junction is Fredley Manor. On the right now is Juniper Hall Field
Studies Centre.

Turn left almost immediately after turning into Headley Road to
follow a chalk track fairly steeply up over the downs, through what
is mostly a wooded landscape rather than open grassland. Stay on the
route rather than being distracted by any side paths until a main
crossroads of the paths is reached and there turn left to descend fairly
steeply towards the village. Another route merges on the left but
continue ahead along the grassy path to the road.

Turn left into School Lane and follow it to the end without turning
out and there the route continues as a path through a little public
green.

Turn right into Dell Close and left out of it, back onto the old
London road cum village street. The Running Horses is just ahead on
the right.

Points of Interest

The parish church is Saxon but rebuilt in Victorian times since when
it has collected afresh items of interest, such as the Flemish panels of
about 1600 in the pulpit and the profile sculpture of Queen Victoria
by the Esher sculptor J. Williamson.

66

Pyrford Lock
The Anchor

This is the place to come on a warm sunny day if you would like to spend time out in the countryside, having a good meal and a drink on a waterside patio watching the boats ply up and down the Wey Navigation. In winter it is just as pleasant to stay inside, warm and cosy, watching the rain on the water through the windows. Best of all, for many families, is the separate playroom provided for children. Needless to say, this is a very popular pub and not always the best place to 'get away from it all'. There is plenty of room though, the food service is no slower than elsewhere and is worth waiting for, and you don't even have to hang around within earshot of the bar to claim your order as a loudspeaker system calls you from the waterside.

At the end of what is now the patio once stood stables for the towing horses working the Wey Navigation and the pub, in those days, was a little rural building with oil lamps etc where the bargees could stay overnight if they weren't bedded down in the hay loft over their horses. That's all gone now and the pub rebuilt but the lock is still there, where the one-day-admirals provide added interest.

The majority of meals are home-made and include vegetarian dishes. The specialities change from day to day. There is no separate restaurant and anyone wanting a group booking is requested to arrange it with the manager in advance. They do not have a drink speciality.

67

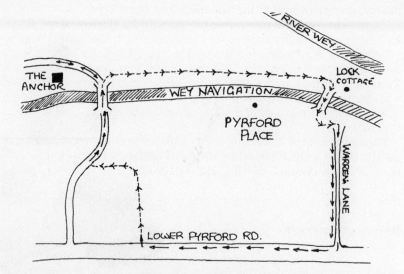

Opening hours: Monday-Friday 11 am-3 pm; 6 pm-11 pm; Saturdays 11 am-11 pm. Sunday 12 noon-3 pm; 7 pm-10.30 pm. Food serving times: Monday-Saturday 12 noon-2.30 pm, 6 pm-9 pm; Sunday 12 noon-1.45 pm, 7 pm-9 pm.

Telephone: 0932 342507.

How to get there: The Anchor is quite close to Wisley Gardens. From the RHS follow the lane away from the A3, through Wisley village, through the savage bends at the farm and so to The Anchor.

Length of the walk: 2½ miles. O.S. Map Landranger Series 187.

Walking off a meal is easy here because it is attractive to walk the towpath, in either direction. That does, however, require coming back the same way. Those who much prefer a circular walk have to accept that part of it must be along the highway, albeit a country road.

The Walk

Leave the pub and walk up to the lock.

Follow the towpath all the way upstream to the next lock (Walsham Gates) which is entirely through countryside. The farmland beyond the trees on the left has been converted to the Wisley Golf Course so the landscaping and the wildlife has changed. Another change involves the demolition of Pyrford Place on the right bank but the

68

historic summerhouse at the waterside has been kept.

Turn right over the packhorse bridge with its shallow steps at the lock but before doing so it is very pleasant to explore the lock area.

Follow the trackway from the bridge, away from the lock. It leads to the highway so beware of letting children and dogs run on ahead. Turn right along Lower Pyrford Lane which runs between the fields with banks of wild flowers but is narrow, so mind the traffic. Look for a public footpath sign on the right (opposite the timber-framed Glebe ·Cottage).

Turn right off the road to follow a path across the fields. These are usually full of vegetables; when the canal opened London's vegetable fields were in country districts like Vauxhall!

Turn left at the T-junction and follow the route to the edge of the field and Lock Lane. Turn right along Lock Lane back to The Anchor.

Points of Interest

Pyrford Place. The lands belonged to Newark Priory, a little further ahead, and at the Dissolution of the Monasteries became royal property, visited by Elizabeth I and her Court. She did not flirt with the poet John Donne here, as local tradition has it, but his early life at the time of his marriage was spent here; an interesting story for winter reading.

Walsham Gates (lock) is at the point where the waters of the river Wey crash off over a great weir to leave a calm flow to continue ahead as the Wey Navigation, until the two merge once more at Weybridge to finish the last stretch to the river Thames. Note the water is level through the Gates; they are only closed to divert flood waters over the weir to safeguard the Navigation. The gates themselves have a rare paddle system, found only here and on the ones upstream at Worsfold Gates, which are thought to be of the original design installed in 1652. They are thus the oldest surviving design in Britain. When the canal was worked by horse power the horses were speeded up along the towpath just used so that they could be unhooked at the last minute to leave the barges free to propel themselves across the pool ahead under their own momentum; a tricky job involving putting the towing rope round a pulley so that the horses pulled back in the other direction rather than plunge into the pool. From the weir note the steps hidden in the bank below the lock cottage; from there the lock keeper used to boat the schoolchildren of Lower Pyrford across to Ripley village school when floods made the usual route impassable. Flood control measures in the 1930s ended the rowboat service.

Godalming
The Ram

The Ram is a special place. It fills visitors with expectation as they see it ahead, a bold black-and-white timber-framed house from the 16th century, perched up on the bank. Bear right in front of it to find the car park. Then the massive garden comes into view, newly planted with less common trees like good old fashioned walnuts. The house used to serve as the local shop, selling wares from the main parlour and selling cider too. That tradition is still maintained as far as the cider is concerned for this is still a real Cider House, not just a pub of that name. There are 35 different ciders to choose from so if you think you don't like cider maybe you haven't found the right one yet. In cold weather they will serve it mulled too. There is of course a range of beers etc but note well, there is NO lager. The food is out of the ordinary too: home-made and what the landlord calls 'an exciting range, constantly being updated'. You can have Tipsy Beef Stew in a Hat, the hat being a Yorkshire pudding the size of a dinner plate, or Pheasant Creole which is half a pheasant on saffron rice with a sauce of pineapple, baby corn, red and green peppers. Vegetarian? Yes, there's plenty of that (after all the headquarters of the World-Wide

Fund for Nature is just round the corner!). There's Stilton Cauliflower Flan or good old Cheese, Leek and Potato Pie. The list is bewildering, some foreign and some traditional British, like rabbit, venison and wild boar. They will take group bookings although there is no separate restaurant at the moment but it's a good place to eat outside when the weather permits. In summer The Ram offers an extensive barbecue service.

Opening hours: Monday-Saturday 11 am-2.30 pm; 6 pm-10.30 pm. Sunday 12 noon-3 pm; 7 pm-10.30 pm. Telephone: 0483 421093.

How to get there: From beside The Wharf runs Catteshall Lane round to Catteshall lock where the Farncombe Boathouse hires out boats for visitors' own adventures. Off Catteshall Lane and well away from the bustle of the town centre, is The Ram.

Length of the walk: 2¾ miles. O.S. Map Landranger Series 186.

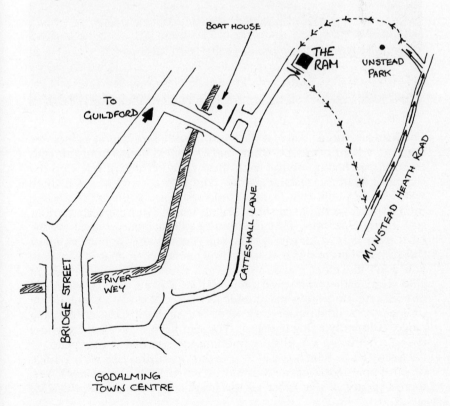

The ramble is simply up the hill, along the top, down to the Navigation and back along the towpath and very pleasant it is too.

The Walk

Bear left out of the pub to follow the lane up but first, note the ram or hydraulic water pump in the bank opposite. It dates from the 1920s and was made by John Blake Ltd of Accrington. Its purpose is to raise water to places up the hillside.

Follow the lane until it becomes a track and then continue up that. Note the entrance to Catteshall Manor on the right – one of several small manors carved out of the large Godalming Manor in the early Middle Ages. Then the king leased this one out to the servant responsible for his linen and laundry. The choice may reflect Godalming's importance for textiles.

On the left note the splendid Tudor timber-framed house, one bay longer than was usual in Surrey. This too is thought to have had connections with the textile industry.

Follow the track all the way up the hill. It's a long steady climb, wonderful in spring with all the woodside wild flowers in bloom. Quietness can be rewarded with sightings of foxes, deer and rabbits.

Turn left when the road is reached. It's a quiet country lane through the trees, very relaxing after the climb and very attractive when dappled with shadows. Look out for 'Orchards' (1899) on the right: one of the most important houses by Sir Edwin Lutyens, who has many associations with this district.

Look right when the lane eventually runs out of the trees, for expansive views eastwards. Then, as the lane starts to rise again look for the driveway to Unstead Park on the left.

Turn left up the Unstead Park driveway and nearer the main gateway follow the signposted footpath to the right. After plunging through the trees it will open out and drop downhill to the Wey valley again, with more good views, especially in winter when the trees are bare. Remember to look back for views of the Park House. Built about 1780, it is considered one of the best of the smaller mansions of that date.

Ignore temptations to take paths off to the right. The path joins a track and by following that the rambler will be guided back round the lower parts of the hillside, on to the quiet access road that leads back to The Ram again.

Brockham
The Royal Oak

The Royal Oak (Allied Breweries) is sandwiched between other old buildings looking out across the village green to the church. It's a grand place to sit outside on a sunny day. Inside it is comfortable and welcoming with home-made food from a menu which changes daily. There is no separate restaurant but they will nevertheless cater for group bookings. As for children and dogs, the response was 'Yes, but both on leads!'

Opening hours: Monday-Saturday 11 am-3 pm; 6 pm-11 pm. Sunday 11 am-3 pm; 7 pm-10.30 pm. Food served: Tuesday-Thursday 7 pm-9 pm, Friday to Saturday 7 pm-9.30 pm, and every lunchtime 12 noon-2 pm.

Telephone: 0737 843241.

How to get there: Brockham lies just south of the A25 to the east of Dorking, with the lane from the main road dipping down to bridge the river Mole and then shooting up to the village green, whereon each November are held particularly splendid Guy Fawkes celebrations.

Parking: There is parking available round the village green.

Length of the walk: 4 miles. O.S. Map Landranger Series 187.

Brockham is arguably the most scenic village in Surrey. From the group of mellow old houses and pub by the village pump a great expanse of green sweeps the eye off to the south where the view is punctuated by the church spire.

This pleasant ramble is along the valley of the Mole to the next village of Betchworth and back again on the other side; the routes used by the villagers to attend Betchworth church before Brockham was provided with its own church in the 19th century. It is also one of the few places in the Mole valley where ramblers can walk very far along the riverside itself, although winter floods ensure the path is well back for most of the route.

The Walk

Turn left out of the pub and follow the building line for a sighting of the old chapel (possibly the oldest in Surrey) and then cut across the green towards the church spire. Pass to the left of the church, following the little path round. Turn left at the road to follow Wheelers Lane.

Turn left on to an unsurfaced road between Wheelwright Cottage and Way House Cottage. The public footpath is indicated on a stone block against the hedge of Wheelwright Cottage.

Follow this route until it eventually forks and there take the left branch. This will go uphill and then twist and turn along until a stile is reached on the left.

Cross the stile and proceed ahead over a field with fine views down to the river Mole or across to the Downs. The large house is Betchworth House and is of architectural importance and of local history interest.

Bear left at the fence and follow the waymarked route along beside it, down to the woods.

Cross the stile into the woods and follow the path to cross a stile out of the woods into hawthorn scrub, emerging into a field and heading for a stile on the far side.

Cross the stile into The Street, Betchworth, and turn left. Proceed to the attractive bridge over the river Mole and on up past Betchworth House (on left) to The Dolphin pub on the right. Turn left onto a signposted footpath opposite The Dolphin and go through the church grounds, keeping to the left path, and through the gate.

Proceed along the footpath with a farm on the right, through two gates and then two split fences and so towards the gardens on the outskirts of Brockham. There are fine views down an enormous drop to the river Mole (try a detour down the 46 steps!).

Turn right onto a gravel track at the junction of paths and so to Kiln Lane. Turn left and follow down to the river bridge and so to Brockham Green, with The Royal Oak on the left at the top of the rise.

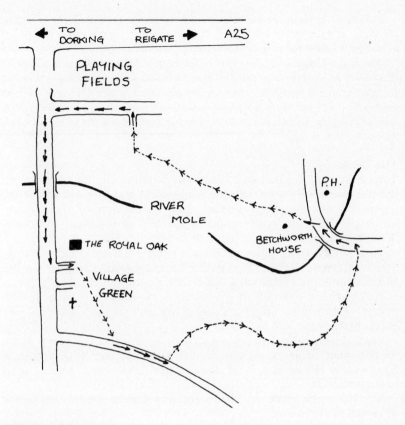

Points of Interest

Brockham church was built in 1846 through the generosity of local benefactors. The architect was Benjamin Ferrey who worked on a number of Surrey churches, with a good eye for creating the something that would add to the landscape. That shows so well here at Brockham. His interiors, however, are disappointing and that too is especially clear here but in all fairness to Ferrey the money was running out by the time he reached the inside and so the original plans were modified.

Betchworth House is one of only five good examples of Carolean architecture in the whole county; built in 1634 it was extended in the 18th and 19th centuries. It is the manor house and the manor has the distinction of only having been up for sale twice since 1088.

Merstham
The Feathers

The Feathers (Ind Coope) is on the roadside (north/London bound carriageway of the A23) by the bend and has its own large car park. Inside it is pleasant enough for a stop, with the usual range of drinks and a menu of home-made food. The house special changes daily.

Opening hours: Monday-Friday 11 am-2.30 pm, 5.30 pm-11 pm. Saturday 12 noon-11 pm. Sunday 12 noon-10.30 pm. Food served daily: 12 noon-2.30 pm. Monday-Friday 5.30 pm-10 pm.

Telephone: 0737 642498.

How to get there: Merstham is on the main A23 London-Brighton road between Redhill and the M25.

Length of the walk: 2¼ miles. O.S. Map Landranger Series 187.

Here on the edge of the Downs is a good place to stop for anyone travelling the rather grim main road across the county. It doesn't look a very likely spot yet a few yards from the highway begins one of the county's most famous village streets, beyond that a footway leads to one of its notable medieval churches and then this ramble takes the explorer for a taste of the hillside pastures and trees, summer flowers and butterflies.

The Walk

Turn left out of the pub and follow the road round to the cul-de-sac called Quality Street.

Explore this to the end, noting aged buildings such as the Old Forge on the right opposite North Cottage dated 1609.

Take the footpath (signposted) from the right side (looking up) next to the Old Forge. Follow this out of the hamlet and over the footbridge spanning the M25 deep in its cutting which thankfully absorbs a lot of the noise, and so to the lane, Gatton Bottom. A bottom in Surrey means a valley! Cross the lane to enter the churchyard.

Leave the churchyard by the east entrance with the lych gate where in early times the funeral services took place; lych is Saxon for corpse. This particular lych gate was fashioned out of a windmill, hence the extra mortices. Feel the central post – it's metal! Note the millstones under your feet.

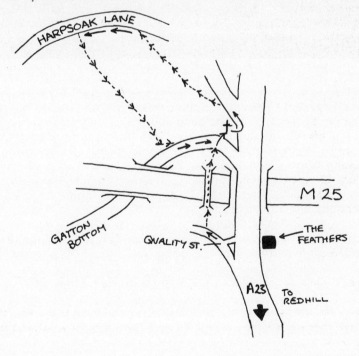

Turn left out of the gate and round to the left to climb Church Hill Road and near the crown of the hill turn left onto a grassy footpath (signposted).

Follow this route up the downs to rejoin the surfaced road which is now Harpsoak Lane.

Turn left to follow the narrow winding country lane for ½ mile to turn left into an unsurfaced road and after a couple of hundred yards turn off left onto a footpath across the field. Follow the path to join with an unsurfaced road and thence to the highway whereupon turn left, which is Gatton Bottom again. Follow this for ½ mile to reach the church again and retrace your route back over the motorway to Quality Street.

Points of Interest

Quality Street gets its unusual name from the play by J.M. Barrie, of Peter Pan fame, from when its leading performers were Sir Seymour Hicks and his wife Ellaline Teriss who lived in the Old Forge at the top of the street. There is a grand mixture of old buildings down both sides, spanning 500 years, some with unusual architectural features hidden within them but they all wear their age so lightly that the scene is deceptive. The whole street is so carefully maintained, with little front gardens and grassy verges that it has been likened to a Hollywood film set of what Americans think an English village should look like. Certainly there is nowhere else in Surrey with this look.

The churchyard: much of interest, especially the architecture of the church which was obviously built by masons and not the village builder. This is no surprise as Merstham was a medieval centre of stone quarrying; even the king had quarries here. Its 'Reigate firestone' was used to build Westminster Palace, Old St. Paul's, London Bridge and Windsor Castle. The west doorway of the tower is the one piece of great quality not to miss and note that the original dragon-head iron hinges are still in use on the door itself.

The church is beautiful inside with a range of interesting items. The most unusual is perhaps a modern memorial brass on the south wall perpetuating the medieval idea. It shows a First World War soldier in uniform. Beside it are two original infants' brasses, one showing the baby still wrapped in its chrisom, indicating that he died when less than one month old. There are not many of those in the country.

Reigate
The Bell

Although it looks small, the street facade of The Bell is deceptive. Step inside and you will find it stretches right back. On the wall are press cuttings testifying to the high quality of its food and customer appreciation. The compilers of a guide to good pub food had just visited ahead of us too. It's home-made food on a set menu with the house specialities changing daily. When asked about drink specialities the landlord didn't enthuse over the beers as most did but drew attention to the selection of house spirits. There isn't room for a separate restaurant in this old building so tables are spread through the pub and children are allowed in to use these for meals. Larger groups must therefore expect to be split up but group bookings are still welcome and when asked how many they could accommodate the landlord jested that they had squeezed in 24 recently. So all in all you will gather that this is a popular pub and that it is advisable to arrive early if you want a table and a seat! Note they serve food an hour earlier than most pubs in this book.

Opening hours: Monday-Saturday 11 am-11 pm. Sunday 12 noon-3 pm; 7 pm-10.30 pm. Food served: Monday-Saturday 11 am-9 pm; Sunday 12 noon-2.15 pm.

Telephone: 0737 24438.

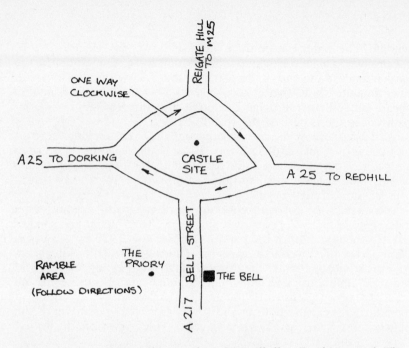

How to get there: Reigate lies on the A25 Redhill to Dorking road. The Bell is in Bell Street which runs out southwards from the one way system to the lowest level of the town.

Length of the walk: 1½ miles. O.S. Map Landranger Series 187.

To the south of Reigate Hill, a beauty spot of renown, lies the old castle town of Reigate. Little that is old remains of the castle except its great mound, or indeed of the medieval town. Nevertheless its contortion of streets and range of buildings are not unattractive and down by the old Priory there is a beautiful park kept in its natural state just waiting to be explored in this quiet walk.

The Walk

Turn left on leaving The Bell and then cross Bell Street to enter the park through its car park entrance.

Cross the car park to pass through a gate keeping the school building on your left.

Continue ahead over the grass. Suddenly the town has been left behind in favour of a grassy vale, sweeping ahead to the west and up the slopes to their wooded tops, to the south.

Look ahead for the willow fringed pond and head for that, aiming to skirt it to the right. This is a popular spot with both people and

80

wildlife. The water can be thick with wildfowl.

Continue in an anti-clockwise direction round to the left before the garden fence at the end of the park and thus follow the (muddy) path over the little bridge that crosses the outfall from the pond. Continue ahead rather than following the pond and thereby join a broader pathway in the fringes of the woodland.

Turn left to follow the pathway through the trees, keeping the main woodland on your right. This too can be a muddy route. Turn right after some 200 yards onto a side path that leads off uphill through the woods. This is fairly steep and the last 50 yards is more than that as it climbs up through a gully.

Turn left at the top and continue along the path, heading for a marker stone that will soon come into view. This 'high point' marker records the donation of the park to the public in 1920 by the Vagan family, to be preserved in its quiet naturalness. Follow the path ahead, past the stone, and enjoy the downhill gradient, bearing left to avoid the large pink house that will come into view, and another gully will lead back downhill towards the grassland again.

Fork right near the bottom and head across the grass towards the playing area with the car park beyond. Fine views of the Priory. Return to the start.

Points of Interest

The priory (now school) founded in 1235, was for the Augustinians and was in use until closed by Henry VIII in 1535 at the Dissolution of the Monasteries. In 1541, in exchange for other properties, he granted it to Lord William Howard who was raised to the peerage as 1st Baron Howard of Effingham for leading the defence of London during Wyatt's Rebellion. He was the father of the Howard of Effingham of Armada fame during the reign of Elizabeth I.

Visitors walking in the park will find no sign that there was ever a medieval priory here. The site has been rebuilt and now presents to us an impressive Palladian house of 1799. Even the terracotta arms of Elizabeth I are of 1835 and not saved from an earlier phase. Nevertheless it all creates a grand English scene, especially when viewed from the formal rose garden in the front.

Shamley Green
The Bricklayers Arms

The Bricklayers Arms is welcoming and comforting within its cream plastered walls and suggestion of old beams. Being served by three breweries brings no surprise that the pub is proud of its range of beers. The menu is large with plenty of variety too and there is a separate eating area which will take group bookings of up to 20. There is a play area in the garden for children.

Opening hours: Monday-Friday 11.30 am-2.30 pm; 5.30 pm-11 pm. Saturday 11.30 am-11 pm. Sunday 12 noon-3 pm; 7 pm-10.30 pm. Food served daily.

Telephone: 0483 898377.

How to get there: Shamley Green lies on the B2128 to the south of Guildford. The Bricklayers Arms will be found by the edge of the green.

Length of the walk: 2½ miles. O.S. Map Landranger Series 186.

This is one of Surrey's most attractive villages. It's a very domestic scene without even the usual complement of the church, which is up on the hill behind. Indeed there are hills all around the village and the following ramble goes up and over one of them to enjoy the views and get the feel of this particular district. The way the character changes every few miles in Surrey is one of the wonders of such a small county.

The Walk

Turn right out of the Bricklayers Arms and follow the road along beside one of the greens to take the first right into a signposted footpath on the right hand side of a private drive.

Follow the path round the boundary of a private garden and cross the stile and continue ahead with pasture on right. (Ignore the stile on the right unless you want to detour off to visit the parish church.) Follow the surfaced road downhill when the route merges with it.

Turn left at the bottom into Woodhill Lane but after a few yards turn off right up a sandy signposted footpath and follow it uphill beside the bank with grassland on the left for quite a long way. Bear left when a path merges from right. The uphill climb is now worth the effort as views open out over the surrounding countryside and down onto the villages.

Cross the stile and bear left to follow a well worn path downhill (steep). No doubt ramblers will pause at this stile to enjoy the views again.

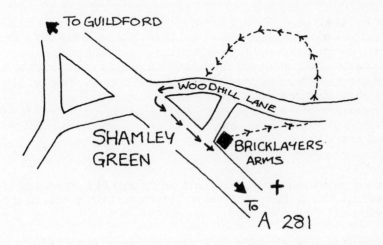

Cross a stile near the bottom of the hill and turn left onto a surfaced driveway.

Turn right onto Woodhill Lane and take the left fork which returns you to the green and the Bricklayers Arms.

Points of Interest

Shamley Green was not created out of the parish of Wonersh until 1881 but the large collection of timber-framed buildings shows there was a thriving community here from the 15th-17th centuries. In those days this was a community of weavers for the local textile industries. The fashionable brick facades added in the 18th century testify to the success of local enterprise and continue the building story up to the Victorian cottages. Not all the half-timbered buildings were built as dwellings; some were originally barns and have been converted.

The old houses: Even if you don't think you are interested in architecture the beautiful array of homes here is bound to catch your eye and before long you're going to be wondering about the age of one or other and so here are the dates of the oldest parts of some (provided by the Shamley Green History Society). Remember they have been added to or altered subsequently. The earliest is 'Lee Crouch' off the green on the Guildford side but around the green: –

Potters, just after 1400 – fine four-bay open hall house.

Easteds, second half of the 16th century.

Arthurs Cottage, early 17th century.

Arthurs, late 16th century.

Former Congregational Chapel, 1900.

Quoin Cottage, 17th century; sometime chapel of rest.

Timbers, used for meetings before the chapel was built.

Red Lion Cottages, Victorian like the pub except the early 17th century one at the right hand end.

Forge Cottage, 1847.

Court House, 16th century; almost certainly a weaving house as there is extra framing inside from which to hang the looms.

Round the corner towards the church is an impressive group with the name Plonks, yes, Plonks, which is thought to come from 'planks' – perhaps it was originally weatherboarded.

Chipstead
The White Hart

The White Hart is well away from residential centres, out on its own with fields and farms for neighbours but easy to find along the main road at Chipstead (with a good sized car park). If you've been before then try it again because at the time of writing (1991) there was a new (very friendly) landlord intent on improving the White Hart. Thus a new dining area is to be created and the kitchens refurbished and when all is completed home-made house specialities are planned for the menu. The garden was being landscaped at the time of going to press.

Drinkwise there is Real Ale as well as IPA and bottled beers and if you arrive on the last Monday of the month you can enjoy the Monthly Quiz. No children inside in the evenings.

Opening hours: Monday-Friday 12 noon-3 pm; 5.30 pm-11 pm. Saturday 12 noon-11 pm. Sunday 12 noon-3 pm; 7 pm-10.30 pm. Food served Monday-Saturday 12 noon-2.30 pm. None available Sunday.

Telephone: 0737 552708.

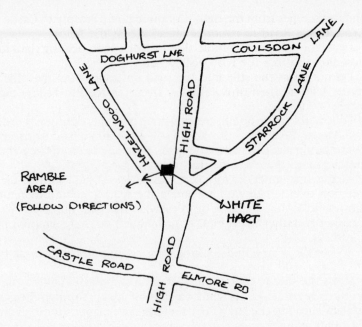

How to get there: Chipstead lies just off the B2032 Coulsdon to Walton on the Hill road.

Length of the walk: 3 miles. O.S. Map Landranger Series 187.

A scattering of farms and small villages grew up among the folds of the high chalk downland of North East Surrey and that's the way it stayed for hundreds of years. Only with the development of the railways did the valleys get opened up and places like Caterham developed into small towns. Quiet places like Croydon, once a country retreat of the Archbishops of Canterbury, expanded more dramatically. In between all this there is still the great rolling countryside of fields and woods with the same scattering of habitations. Chipstead is one of these; a place by name but with little sense of location as there is still no village as such around the church.

This lovely ramble is an up-and-down exploration of the downland, through woods and fields.

The Walk

Turn right out of the pub and cross the road immediately to turn left along the signposted footpath. It takes you between field fences to pass between the old buildings ahead.

Continue ahead, downhill along a surfaced path and bear left when another merges from the right. Continue down steeply to Castle Road. Cross Castle Road to continue ahead across the field.

Cross the stile and continue along a worn path, bearing right to walk downhill towards the road visible below.

Do not cross the stile into the road but follow the roadside fence to the left and then turn left away from the road to follow the next series of footpath signs.

Follow the path uphill, bearing round to the right away from the field landscape into scrub. Cross a stile back into a field landscape and continue ahead. The path soon bears right and leads off into the trees and becomes quite a wide trackway.

At the first junction fork left onto a lesser path and at the next junction turn left downhill, leaving the woods behind in return for more fields. After a snatch of trees again the path meets the road on a corner so rather than think of turning left or right, simply proceed ahead.

Follow the road uphill, looking for a signposted footpath on the left after about 100 yards.

Cross the stile to follow the footpath through the field to the track on the other side. Turn right along the trackway, through the gate and straight ahead to the High Road, emerging opposite a football ground. Turn left along the wide grassy verge beside a field.

Turn left onto the first signposted footpath, through a scrubby patch into another field and keep right all the way down the side of the field.

Turn right at the bottom and so out onto the road, which is Castle Road again, and turn left. Look out for the path on the right from which the ramble emerged earlier and from there retrace the route to the pub.

Elstead
The Woolpack

The Woolpack is a reminder that this district was once the centre of a woollen textile industry and is still one of the larger buildings in the village, on the main road linking to the east with the A3 at Milford. There's a good friendly welcome and specialities like the 'Old English and Colonial' menu and beer served straight from the barrels into the glasses. The food is home-made and can be taken in the separate restaurant although they do not take reservations. There is a family room at the rear near the garden and on site car parking.

Opening hours: 11 am-2.30 pm; 6 pm-11 pm Monday-Saturday. 12 noon-3 pm and 7 pm-10.30 pm Sunday. Food served: 12 noon-2 pm and 7 pm-9.45 pm Monday-Saturday; 12 noon-2 pm and 7.30 pm-9 pm Sunday.

Telephone: 0252 703106.

How to get there: Elstead lies on the B3001 between Farnham and Milford.

Length of the walk: 3½ miles. O.S. Map Landranger Series 186.

This is heathland countryside down in the south west of the county and this ramble has been chosen to introduce just that, so it is mostly rural, without a range of old buildings that can be found using the other suggestions in this book. Much of the heathland is reserved for military use but this ramble skirts the edge of those territories and is therefore perfectly safe.

The Walk

Turn left out of The Woolpack and follow the road round to the left. The pavement changes to the right hand side of the road (Apple Tree Cottage is just one of the preserved cottages in this old village).

At the junction bear left rather than turning right at the little green, although the church opposite is worth a visit. Continue along the street with the church on the right.

Turn left immediately after the school on the left, down Red House Lane, as far as the entrance to Red House Farm at which point turn right onto a signposted bridleway, which will go through mixed woodland and remnants of the heathland which it is invading. Keep on this route rather than taking any of the side options. Continue ahead at the crossroads in the paths.

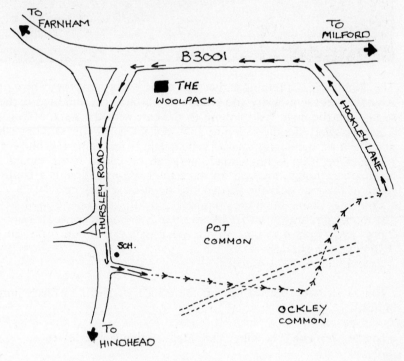

Turn left at the T-junction at the bottom of the slope in the wooded area. Continue ahead at the crossroads in paths, in the woods but open heathland now comes up on the right.

Take the left option when the path splits into three, to go up the hill through the wood. Here will be found warning signs that the route crosses one of Surrey's military training areas. Be prepared for unexpected noises and soldiers on exercise! Do not pick up strange objects!

Follow the route, which in summer is walled in with thick bracken. Follow along a fence on the left with pasture beyond and downhill through the trees; this can be wet in winter.

Turn left on to Hookley Lane and follow to the next junction which is the B3001 Farnham-Elstead-Milford road. Turn left on to this and return through the village housing to Elstead centre (The Woolpack is on your left).

Points of Interest

The parish church is a small medieval building heavily Victorianised in 1871. Nevertheless, the 15th century east window remains and has led observers to guess that its high quality comes from the masons of Winchester Cathedral because Elstead was a chapelry of Farnham, home of the bishops. Even rarer is the medieval wooden doorcase for the north door and the way the door arches were created by splitting one curved tree trunk into two. Occasionally the door to the bellchamber is open to reveal the medieval stair with its treads simply notched out of a tree trunk. The internal timber frame for the bell tower is worth noting, for comparison with Thursley, if that ramble is being walked too.

It was at the little green outside the church that George V left the royal car to continue on horseback down the little lane to the side to review his troops on Hankley Common, during the First World War. It was a proud moment for the people of Elstead. His route can still be followed as an added extra on this ramble, as the lane leads down to the attractive hamlet of Westbrook (retrace route after visit).

Ewhurst
The Bull's Head

The Bull's Head is a brick pub dated 1908 under cream-washed plaster darkened with ivy. It's pleasant inside – with a suggestion of old beams, wildlife pictures and a bull's head at one end of the bar. All of the food is home-made and there are several chef's specials. Among their selection of beers is the Friary Meux special Sussex Bitter.

Opening hours: Monday-Saturday 11 am-2.30 pm, 6 pm-11.30 pm, Sunday 12 noon-3 pm, 7 pm-10.30 pm. Food served 11 am-2.30 pm, 6 pm-10 pm Monday to Saturday; 12 noon-2.30 pm, 7 pm-10 pm Sunday.

Telephone: 0483 277447.

How to get there: Ewhurst is on the B2127 to the east of Cranleigh.

Length of the walk: 3 miles. O.S. Map Landranger Series 187.

Ewhurst is a twist of street out in the clay lands to the south of Leith Hill. It was all forest from which farms were cut out and that is still the basic pattern today. It is a very different landscape from many parts of Surrey, close and green and sometimes noticeably wet. The village itself has fewer old buildings than many but

91

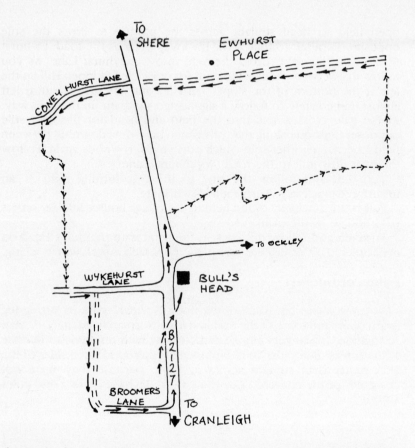

those at the church entrance catch the eye and the church itself is a beautiful Norman building.

This pleasant walk is through woods and fields that are typical of this region but they can be muddy so it may be best to keep the ramble until after the pub visit. There are plenty of other routes around here for anyone wishing to make a return visit; it's beautiful in May — bluebell time.

The Walk

Turn right out of the pub and cross the road junction to go straight ahead up the lane (Shere Road) which leads out of the bend. Turn right at the first signposted footpath, into woodland, and at the end turn right over a stile into pasture. Follow the path and cross the next stile and continue into the woodland, crossing another stile to trudge steeply up hillside, still in the woods. Cross a stile on the left into an open field to head straight across the pasture to cross the stile opposite. Turn left to follow the trackway as far as the road. Ewhurst Place is on the right. Cross the road into Coneyhurst Lane. As you follow this between houses look out for one called Shippen Hill on the left at the bottom of the slope. Turn left into its drive to turn left almost immediately to follow a signposted footpath up the trackway. At the gate cross a stile into the field and head for the next stile opposite. Continue along the path which now runs downhill between field fences to another stile which puts you into woods again. Follow the path downhill to the road (Wykehurst Lane).

Turn left and follow the lane to the first turning right – an unsurfaced trackway. Turn right down there.

Follow the trackway round behind the village houses into Broomers Lane and so to the main road.

Turn left and follow this back to the bend with the Bull's Head on the corner. This passes the parish church which is well worth seeing.

Points of Interest

The parish church has some of the finest Norman work in Surrey (eg south door) and some of the best imitation Norman from the Victorian restoration. It's all very simple and pleasing with refinements like the 17th century altar rails. These, unusually, run round three sides of the altar rather than straight across in front, because they were not designed for the church. They came from Baynards Park a few miles away.

Old Coulsdon
The Fox

You can fortify yourself for the ramble with a good meal here. The same lady has been preparing the meals for 25 years; and needless to say part of the menu is her own home-made selection comprising in all a large variety. There is a separate restaurant, taking group bookings up to 20 in which children are welcome during restaurant hours, otherwise there is a special children's garden. No dogs please. For drinks there is no particular house speciality, just the usual range of beers.

Opening hours: Monday-Saturday 11 am-3 pm; 5 pm-11 pm. Sunday 12 noon-3 pm; 7 pm-10.30 pm. Food served: Monday-Saturday 12 noon-2.30 pm; Sunday 12 noon-2 pm.

Telephone: 0883 344643.

How to get there: The Fox is situated just off Coulsdon Common backing on to Farthing Downs and even the building is green!

Length of the walk: 2 miles. O.S. Map Landranger Series 186.

Enjoy the Downs on this top edge of Surrey. Londoners have come out to do so for generations and it still isn't spoilt — the hills and valleys take a lot of beating!

The Walk

Turn left out of the car park, down Fox Lane, looking for the entrance to the common on the right. The common is grassy rather than of heather and gorse as found in other parts of Surrey.

Cross the grassland diagonally left and bear left at the fork to go downhill towards the trees.

Follow the path between the trees onto a trackway to be followed all the way down to the bottom of this — The Happy Valley. There's plenty of hawthorn on either side so the wildlife is rich.

Turn right at the T-junction of the routes at the bottom of the valley, to travel further along the bottom of the valley for ½ mile or so.

Turn left into the trees where the footpath is signposted to Hooley and Devilsden Wood and then left at the fork. The next section goes

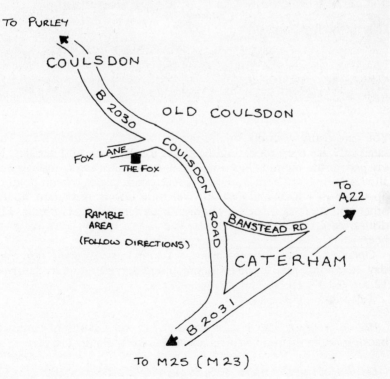

uphill steeply to the T-junction, at which, turn left. This direction is signposted once again to Happy Valley. Bear right at the next fork and straight ahead up through more woodland. Turn left at the cross junction and left again at the next junction to go slightly downhill to emerge from the trees at the top of the valley.

Turn right once out of the trees, through a small wooded area and once through that turn left down a track with a woodchip surface to the valley bottom and turn left and diagonally across to the right to climb the opposite hillside by the worn path through the grass. It's steep!

Bear right at the fork and then right along a path into the trees. Stay on this path, ignoring sidepaths, until it emerges from the trees on the top of the common and bear right. Now the starting point on the common has come back into view and so retrace your route to the pub.